Intentional Aging

7 Practical Actions
to Live Well and
Minimize the Risk of Dementia

Jeannette Franks, Ph.D.
Based on Dr. Franks' talks
'7 Actions to Take to Stay Out of a Nursing Home'

ISBN 979-8-218-11728-3

Cover artwork: Blue Spiral on Light by Patty Harrold. Painted at Elderwise, whose mission is to enrich the lives of caregivers and adults living with dementia through teaching and demonstrating the Elderwise philosophy and practice of Spirit-Centered Care. Learn more at elderwise.org.

Author photo: Joel Sackett, Bainbridge Island, WA

Book design and interior illustrations: Joy Rubin Creative

Table of Contents

Preface 7

Introduction 9

1. Design for a Lifetime............................ 19
   Universal Design

2. Death with Dignity, or Not—
   Many Choices 43
   End-of-life issues

3. The F Word...63
   Getting your $$$$ together

4. Social Support 73
   Family, friends, and government

5. A Bucket of Wellness Factors 89
   Dementia prevention and health

6. Meaning and Purpose 109
   A well-lived life

7. Interconnected, Interwoven
   Intersections 123
   Action and activism

Resources...133

Acknowledgements 137

To Sundance Rogers, M.D., who saved my life.
Everyone should have a primary care physician as brilliant,
as compassionate, and as conscientious as this doctor
who takes time to listen and ask questions. And everyone
of all ages should have Medicare.

Preface

The background for this book began in the mid-1990s, when I was doing research for my Ph.D. dissertation, *Residents in Long-term Care: A Case-controlled Study of Individuals in Nursing Homes and Assisted Living in Washington State*. I visited dozens and dozens of nursing homes and assisted living communities[1], and interviewed as many as 20 people in each community, resulting in hundreds of interviews. The dissertation was recognized with the 1997 Student Research Award for "Outstanding Research Relevant to Aging and Directly Applicable to Practice" by the American Society on Aging.

With this foundation of knowledge, I found a publisher that was interested in a guide to state-wide retirement communities. The industry was booming, and little was known about specific communities, other than the enthusiastic paid advertising. I published *Washington Retirement Options: The Statewide Guide to Independent and Assisted Living Communities*. This wordy title took me to 52 cities and towns in Washington State, some with as many as 40 communities (Seattle) or as few as one or two in each of them.

I learned personally that an age-segregated community was not a good fit for me. My spouse and I always had friends and neighbors of all ages. As a professor, I respected the insights and diversity of graduate students in their 20s, 30s, 40s and 50s. We can

---

[1] Nursing homes are federally- and state-regulated 'skilled care' facilities. Assisted living, in most states, is basically room and board with housekeeping and some activities, plus perhaps, transportation.

always learn so much from each other.

And I knew that if at all possible, I did not want to end my days in a nursing home. I paid attention to those who died at home or in a retirement community. There were commonalities, sadly not the least of which was money. So many people find their retirement funding dwindling to the point of limiting options. Most industrialized countries have robust social services and integrated universal health care that encompass home care options and affordable housing. The United States does not.

I know that most other older people also do not want to end up in a nursing home, other than for short-stay rehabilitation. Survey after survey shows statistics that most older people want to age in place. I do too.

When my most recent book came out, *To Move or to Stay Put*, I did a series of talks at senior centers, libraries, social groups on "Seven Ways to Stay Out of a Nursing Home." I learned much from the audiences—what they knew and what they didn't know; what I knew and what I didn't know.

This book is a result of that process. We want to age intentionally and avoid ending up in a situation we do not like.

Introduction

Do you visualize dying in a nursing home? Tubed up in intensive care? I don't. My goal is to live well until I die, and I suspect that the reason you are holding this book in your hands is that is your goal too. Its underlying purpose is to help you plan ahead to lessen the risk of ending your days in pain and suffering, or so compromised that you cannot communicate with those you love. So, let's start with this: *Imagine a good death for yourself.* But, in order to achieve that goal, we have to start with living well in the present.

Although everyone defines living well differently, and it is difficult to measure objectively, it certainly implies mutual kindness and respect, control, contributing to society, and not compromising the happiness of family, friends, and caregivers.

In my professional life, I chose to follow the path of gerontology, not because it is popular or glamorous (obviously, it isn't). I wanted to be of service, and I wanted to be in a position to teach others about aging and older people as well. But, even for a Ph.D. gerontologist who has spent decades writing and teaching about aging and having done research on long-term care, getting old sneaks up on you. I am surprised at what is happening to me in my early 70s. The people I love the most die. Even with two titanium hips, I am not nearly as fast, as flexible, and as active as I was even just ten years ago. ("Just"—did I ever think I would call ten years ago "just" ten years ago?)

Seeing my once-lively grandfather wither in a traditional nursing home was one impetus that put me on this path. Working at Community Services for the Blind was another. Primarily old and female visually impaired people had few options for skills training, home-delivered services, disability-friendly infrastructure, and other crucial resources. I learned early in my career that those without sight, or without good vision, of course work and play, have careers and families, lead lives like anyone else. But if you are old and blind and poor, your opportunities for a meaningful and joyful life are limited. The lives of single women of color are especially limited. Racism and ageism are a double struggle.

My beloved grandfather ended his days in an expensive, enlightened, and caring nursing home. He hated it. The staff was kind and capable. Their only complaint of him was when he occasionally grabbed at their breasts. This was in the 1970s, when, in my opinion, some nursing homes were better funded and cared for people not as severely disabled and demented as is often the case today. The staff was, as far as I could tell, exemplary.

His death was miserable. My father and I were there constantly, watching him suffer each breath before he died. No one mentioned hospice and we didn't think of it. I don't think there even was a nearby hospice organization at that time.

Today we have more choices, more information, more services, and more modifications that we can make in how we live and, therefore, how we die. Based on a popular talk that I presented to hundreds of people over several years, "7 Actions to Take to Stay out of a Nursing Home," this book tells you about these options. Many ideas, facts, and opinions in the book come from participants at those talks. Some of its emphases are also based on what audiences missed or got wrong. Folks at the talks sometimes said, "Keeping busy," or, "Having a sense of humor," might help you in old age. Perhaps. Those are nice, but the concept of a meaningful life is much more complex than that. It's not about trying to improve your brain by doing puzzles, crosswords, or computerized brain games. There are a few studies that suggest that "engagement in late-life cognitively challenging activity" may be useful, but also read chapter 5 to learn what additional activities evidence suggests may (or may not) lower the risk of dementia.

After drafting much of the book and persuading a few friends and colleagues to read and comment, it is clear that the point is not just to stay out of a nursing home, although that indeed is to be avoided. COVID has proved the importance of avoiding traditional nursing homes. As I write this, at the end of 2020 and through mid-2022, we have witnessed deaths and diagnoses of coronavirus climb, especially in nursing homes. This may be the worst health disaster since the plague in the Middle Ages.

By January 2021, over forty percent of deaths from the virus in the United States had been tied to nursing homes or other long-term care facilities. An April 23, 2020, *Washington Post* article cites the World Health Organization suggestion that "up to half of coronavirus-related deaths in Europe are occurring in long-term-care facilities..." This alone is a good reason to reason to age intentionally and not end your life institutionalized, isolated, and suffering. An assumption, backed up by research and opinion, is that the average perceived quality of life in a nursing home is lower than that of a person not in a nursing home, regardless of age and pandemics.

The good news is that a large percentage, perhaps 80%, of older people never spend more than one or two weeks in skilled care (which is the legal definition of a nursing home), usually in the process of rehabilitation from a hospitalization.

The mission of this book is to improve quality of life in old age. The core values associated with it are that we are interconnected, interdependent, and that old age should not compromise quality of life, respect, dignity, and self-worth. Each chapter focuses on one of seven action areas that you can better understand in order to minimize the risk of spending the last years of your life miserable.

The Seven-Strand Braid

When I was working on my Ph.D., one required course was Research Methods. A useful exercise was to create a diagram or other visual tool to illustrate a theoretical model. For example, Venn diagrams, usually three overlapping circles, are often used to illustrate a concept such as the bio/psycho/social model. Many health analyses use this model to help demonstrate how illness or wellness have biological, psychological, and social components that are interrelated.

Seven circles proved to be too messy for my conceptual model of a high quality of life, which consists of recognizing the importance of Universal Design, Finances, End-of-Life Planning, Social Support, Dementia Prevention, Meaning and Purpose, and a Healthy Planet. Attention to all seven of these intertwining domains cannot but help to improve quality of life at any age, but especially old age. For example, approaching end-of-life issues, and actually experiencing end of life, are inextricably woven with family and friends, medical care, and finances, as well as meaning and purpose.

So, visualize seven colors woven together to form a single braid.

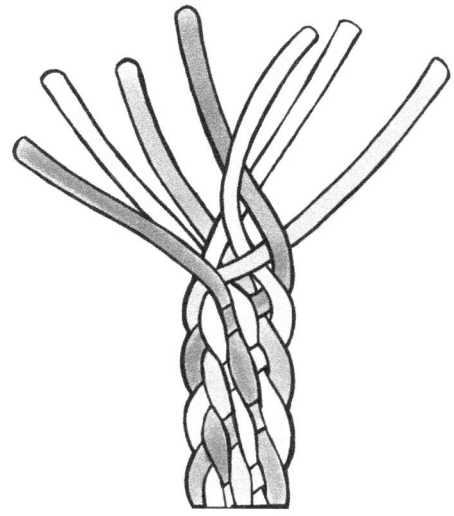

1. **Universal design=blue**
2. **Money=gold (of course)**
3. **End-of-life Planning=red**
4. **Social Support=silver**
5. **Dementia Prevention=purple**
6. **Meaning and Purpose=cyan**
7. **Clean, green planet=green**

The thickness of each strand will be different for each of us. While accessible design is crucial for our last decades, whether or not you have enough money to relocate or remodel deeply impacts whether or not you have an accessible place to live and a good quality of life. The finance strand might be larger for you than for other people, as it will influence your life and choices more if you don't have enough money. Millionaires rarely end up in nursing homes. The corollary of that is, if your old age is not well funded, you are more likely to end up in a situation less to your liking. While having a robust private and governmental social support network, as well as ingenuity and luck, are useful to keep you out of a nursing home, money can also help.

Here are, more precisely, the topics:

1. Design for a lifetime: UD. As I pointed out in a previous book, *To Move or To Stay Put*, it is crucial to find *your* best fit. Many variables, such as geography, proximity of family and friends, your partner's preferences, your budget, aesthetics, your spiritual belief system, etc., all contribute to 'fit.' The right person in the right environment enhances the fit. It's like the perfect pair of jeans—you may never find them. But you may find an appealing solution that you can afford. Especially if you do your homework. This book is part of your homework and the chapter on Universal Design (UD) is part of enhancing the person/environment fit, wherever you are.

2. Die the way you want: While we may not be able to predict when and how we will die, we can be certain that we will. Documenting and disseminating your end-of-life preferences can make your ending more true to your desires and values.

3. Meaning and purpose: From Buddha to Jesus to Mohammed, and perhaps your mother, all thought that you "should do something with your life." That will differ for everyone, but in my opinion, life is not about wealth, or knitting, or being a great cook. It is, for example, about sharing your wealth, clothing the cold, feeding the hungry.

4. Master the F word—Finances. There are few avenues for older people, other than going back to work, to remedy insufficient retirement funds. Economists are lamenting that few boomers have saved enough for retirement. A good example of two strands of our 'braid,' finances and social support, is that the richest country in the world should have a more robust social safety net for people of all ages who fall into poverty—social support isn't just family and friends. Every other developed country has more low-cost or free medical care, housing, home care, etc. for older people than the U.S.

5. Live a healthy life and mitigate the risk of dementia. This is more challenging than it may sound, but current research is abundantly clear: exercise, nutrition, social support, and so much more add not just years, but joy to life. There is also increasing evidence that lifestyle factors may influence the risk of dementia

6. Social support: Foster it. Nurture family and friendships. Revered geriatrician Thomas Perls has a 'longevity calculator' that asks, along with all of the above, "How many close new friends have you made in the last year?"

7. Help create a healthy, peaceful planet: Many different tools to measure quality of life or happiness include the environment. Personally, I believe that the world environment is crucial to aging well and aging in place. We need elder-friendly cities and communities. We need a healthy planet with spacious green forests, clean clear rivers, and delicious safe air. We need to mitigate climate change promptly.

Why this book?

There are many excellent books on home modifications for aging in place. There are books and more books on end-of-life issues. There are books and books and books on exercise! So why read this particular book? Read this book because it brings together these most important issues in a concise, useful way. Why get four or five books on these seven topics when you can use just this one? I have worked to bring the most relevant current information to you in a succinct, readable way.

What this book is *not* is a scholarly treatise, though there is a brief resource list for additional resources and understanding. If you want footnotes and lengthy documentation, this is not your book. If you want new ideas and information, it is.

This is not a book that is anti-aging or ageist. You cannot, nor should you want to, prevent aging. You want to be healthy, attractive, and smart at whatever age you are. Generalizations about any age group will be wrong. When I was teaching, graduate students would sometimes say to me, "I love old people; they are so sweet." Or, "I don't like old people; they are so crabby." Heck, most babies, teenagers, and *all* other ages tend to be sweet *and* crabby, often in the same five minutes. We are all sweet sometimes and crabby sometimes.

If the word ageist does not provoke dismay in you, think of how odious are the clichés, negative stereotypes, and bigotry of people who are sexist or racist. They are despicable. Just like sexism and racism, ageism is awful. It inspires self-loathing, limits potential and opportunities, and is just plain wrong. However, unlike pornography, we often don't 'know it when we see it.' It is *not* a compliment to say, "I love your new hair color; it makes you look younger." It *is* a compliment to say, "You look great."

The U.S. is a societal culture of generational profiling. We generalize about boomers, Millennials, Gen X, and Gen Z. Again, it is a disservice to generalize. If you throw everyone into one category and expect strong similarities, you are bound to be wrong. We can, to a certain extent, generalize about humans when they are first born. There are established bell-shaped curves that establish normalcy for when infants start walking and talking. But the older a human becomes, the more variability there is. Logically, that makes it even less accurate to generalize about old people, who will have even more variability. Yet our culture assigns negative connotations about age. *Senile* and *juvenile* have both come to have derogatory associations, even though they literally only refer to age, such as senile macular degeneration, or juvenile salmon.

You need not read these chapters in the order they are written. You may already be an expert on end-of-life planning, estates, and finances. However, even as an expert, you still may learn something new—or tell *me* about important facts omitted or update information in this fast-changing world. You can contact me through my website, ***jeannettefranks.org.***

Some factors that contribute to a great quality of life in old age are well established. Are you really practicing a healthy lifestyle? Read new tricks and techniques for acquiring healthier habits. Healthy living is more important than ever because we continue to learn more about dementia and how a healthy lifestyle, particularly exercise, can lower your risk of many diseases, including perhaps dementia. Other topics, such as in Chapter One, rarely occur to people until it is too late. So read this book in any order you please, but please learn what you can do in order to lessen the risk of a shortened and more painful life. Age intentionally.

1

Design for a Lifetime, (UD)

How can UD maximize your quality and quantity of life? And what is it?

What's less known but particularly crucial

This book is not starting with the most obvious. Nor with the easiest, or the most difficult. It's most useful to start with what's less known but particularly crucial. This important principle you will be reading about here is one that most people, of all ages, know little or nothing about. Or you might think you are well informed on this subject, but the technology keeps improving, so you may miss significant advances. What are these principles that will help maximize the possibility of aging in place, as opposed to dying miserably in a hospital or nursing home? They are the principles of *universal design* (UD). They apply to homes and communities of all types, but for our purposes, the focus is on intentionally-designed or modified housing—your house, condo, apartment, manufactured home—whatever you prefer for aging in place.

Universal Design is the key

If you've never encountered this term, it's well worth researching and understanding. Universal Design (UD) is a key concept than can preclude injury at best and ending up in a nursing home at worst. UD enables people of almost all ages and abilities to easily use doors, plumbing, walkways, devices, and more, even if vision, hearing, agility, touch, strength, or cognition are compromised. Let's face it. Aging inherently causes change and not always for the better.

The seven principles of Universal Design

It's crucial to master these seven principles. Originally on the website of North Carolina State University, these principals are now found on multiple websites, including the excellent Centre for Excellence in Universal Design in Dublin, Ireland. There are many more, but all embrace these fundamentals:

ONE: Equitable Use.
TWO: Flexibility in Use.
THREE: Simple and Intuitive Use.
FOUR: Perceptible Information.
FIVE: Tolerance for Error.
SIX: Low Physical Effort.
SEVEN: Size and Space for Approach and Use.

Where do you want to live?

Surveys, polls, and questionnaires consistently find that the majority of older people want to age in place. Your living situation will contribute to making that happen, especially if it makes it less likely for you to fall, be in an accident, or be forced out by your well-meaning adult children. But most homes and communities today impede rather than help 'aging in place.' Whether it's a crack in the sidewalk or a little rug that trips you up, breaking a bone can lead to disaster for an older person. After my beloved husband, who had osteopenia, fell, and broke nine ribs, he never got out of intensive care, where he died.

An important predictor of satisfaction in one's last home is how the question, "Who decided you were going to live here?" is answered. Generally, the happiest say, "I did!" If you are determined to stay in your delightful long-time home that has three stories, an inaccessible laundry in the basement, and is miles from a grocery, that is *your* decision. If your adult children demand that you move to be by them or to assisted living, or at the very least to an accessible home, *it's up to you.* There is much that can be done to make a "Peter Pan House" (as if you'll never grow old) much more livable, easier to care for, and safer. Often it is possible to install an elevator or stair lift or make other modifications. Most of this chapter shares insights in how to do so.

A good reason to stay put

One strong reason for staying where you are is dementia. This is the umbrella term used for many types of negative cognitive change associated with aging—Parkinson's, head trauma, Lewy bodies, tranescemic accidents (TIAs), stroke—but perhaps 85% of age-related dementias are Alzheimer's, often in combination with another type of one of the aforementioned dementias.

Most of these dementias usually start with short-term memory loss. A hallmark of Alzheimer's is that the disease progression is very slow, so much so that when asked when it started, family members usually say, "I don't know." It is subtle, slow, and pernicious.

But, because short-term memory loss with Alzheimer's and other dementias is usually so gradual, much long-term memory stays intact for many years— often even more than a decade. If you are still in your familiar home, you know how to manage the kitchen, deal with laundry, and visit with your well-known neighbors. Your long-term memory allows you to continue to be the master of your environment and your social life. But you may *never* master a brand-new environment with people you've never met before in your life, especially without a partner. If you have short-term memory loss, you won't be able to keep information in your short-term memory long enough to process it into long-term memory. This is one of many good reasons for aging in place.

First, a rant

New, purpose-built housing is only just now starting to 'get' aging in place. Although reading this book minimizes, but does not eliminate, your risk of ending up in a dementia-care facility, it is important to grasp the following example.

A large body of well-researched and well-thought-out designs for dementia-friendly residential facilities exists. A prosthetic environment, one that enables users with memory loss to have maximum function, control, and choice, is basically a circular floor plan. When a person exits his or her *private* (that's important) room, whether turning left or right, he or she ultimately ends up in a dining room, preferably where fresh fruit and snacks are available 24/7.

Then, exiting the dining room left or right, eventually the person passes his or her room, with clear signals of home such as a wedding portrait, military photo, or pictures of family children, next to the door to the private apartment. That's *your* family and *your* private room and bathroom. The principles of prosthetic design enable a person with cognitive and/or physical limitations to continue to be master of the home environment to the greatest extent possible. Not only is privacy conducive to calm and harmony, it also mitigates the risk of COVID or other diseases.

Sadly, some builders hire an architect who is the lowest bidder and often wind up with a floor plan that leads every wanderer to the frustration of a locked and/or alarmed door. Often an outdoor area is inaccessible or leads to dead ends. Or allows easy escape. Oops!

Some important principles for your 'forever home'

Smooth, ground level entrances without stairs. One should be able to enter the front door over a minor edge or no edge at all. Even if you don't use a walker or wheelchair, you do have or will have family and friends who find a threshold a serious impediment. If you insist on a multi-story home, start researching elevators and stacking closets (one over the other on each floor) now!

Door handles should be levers that can operate with a closed fist or elbow. These turn out to also be handy if you are trying to keep your hands sterile or hang on to the groceries, or the dog, or the baby.

One should be able to enter the shower over a minor edge, or no edge at all. That is, the level of the floor in and out of the bathroom and shower is the same. Well-placed tiling in the shower moves all water to the drain.

The bathroom floor is non-slip without area rugs. Since cold, bare floors are unpleasant, heated floors may well be worth the splurge.

Cork or bamboo floors are more foot-friendly than tile, which is cold and less forgiving in the case of a fall or dropped teacup.

Ideally the bathroom entry and shower entry are at least 32 inches, wide enough for a wheelchair.

At the very least, a shower stool and a hand-held showerhead within easy reach are essential, as well as plenty of grab bars and towels, also within easy reach.

Higher commodes are safer, and should have sturdy handholds on both sides.

Fixtures should be grabable without coming out of the wall. I'll always remember visiting a person in a hospice residence where I heard this horrendous crash in the bathroom. He had, as many do, used the towel bar as a grab bar. It pulled right out of the wall and he hit the floor like a meat-wrapped stone.

Footwear! In a well-designed study of 1371 adults 65 and older over 2 years, the number of those who fell at home was compared to those who had not fallen. Those who wore sneakers did much better than those in stocking feet or barefoot.

Low pile wall-to-wall carpet, even in a bathroom, has the least risk and is much cheaper to install and replace than the cost of a hospital stay.

Lever light switches you can operate easily with an elbow.

Night lights

Terrifying you with facts

I'm not going to bore you with a bunch of statistics. I'm going to terrify you with facts.

The most dangerous room in the house

The average home bathroom is the most dangerous room in the house. Data indicate that more older people suffer falls and fractures in a bathroom than anywhere else in the home. Falls and fractures can be a one-way trip to the nursing home for an older person. According to the Center for Disease Control (CDC), during the 10 years tracked in a study published in 2018, falls-related deaths among U.S. residents 65 and older rose—in terms of rates of death from falls—to an increase from 47 per 100,000 to 61.6 per 100,000 in that age group. This may be due to the increasing older population, an increased use of medications, lack of exercise, lack of good home design, and probably a combination of all of the above. Falls are the leading cause of injury-related death.

People often say, "I love to soak in the bath." Forget it. It's hard on aging skin and just plain dangerous. You need to have a shower, preferably one large enough for a shower seat and hand-held shower head on a vertical bar that is study and adjustable.

Many studies suggest that a broken hip and subsequent hospitalization is often the first step to the nursing home. A safe, accessible bathroom is one key to staying out of a hospital. A stay in a hospital often precipitates the move to a nursing home. A significant number of people admitted to nursing homes never move out.

Don't wait until *after* you fall down in your bathroom. It's much easier to have the bathroom remodeled the way you want if you're not in the hospital with a broken hip.

Visual accessibility is crucial

Even with the best treatments and optics, and absence of disease, our eyes change with age and not for the better. According to the Center for Disease Control and Prevention (CDC), "The prevalence of blindness and vision impairment increases rapidly with age among all racial and ethnic groups, particularly over the age of 75." Macular degeneration and other irreparable causes of vision loss usually end in some remaining functional vision, which is improved dramatically with appropriate lighting, textural differences, and high contrast, especially kitchens, stairs, and doorways. Look for these:

Magnification tools continue to improve so that computing, reading, sewing, cooking are much easier.

Kurtzweil text-to-speech devices read print aloud.

Podcasts and audio books are easily available, especially with a voice-activated device such as Echo.

Many devices and computers can make print **more accessible with enlargement**.

Lighting and contrast can be particularly important. Increasing light and insisting on high contrast, for example on the leading edge of stairs, is lifesaving. Sturdy contrasting railings are crucial.

Dimmer switches are good energy savers and as a bonus, can decrease glare. You can adjust the lights to your needs—not the architect's.

Home tips—so you don't tip over

How would living in the most appropriate environment for all levels of ability lessen the risk of being miserable in old age? Several stunning reasons emerge.

Living in an accessible home reduces accidents in every room in the house. To repeat, minimizing the risk of falls and fractures is a great way to stay out of a nursing home. We'll talk about balance and exercise later, but having clear, wide, easy-to-see pathways throughout your home is crucial. A minimum two feet wide for a traffic path is recommended and bigger is even better. Good design that goes along with these principals is unobtrusive, elegant, and intuitive. It need not and should not look institutional or medical at all.

Nightlights: Again, the bathroom is the most dangerous room in a home. But an appropriate nightlight can illuminate the commode without blinding your bedmate.

Have drinking water on the nightstand—a good idea to avoid a trip.

Non-slip slippers right where you get out of bed are smart.

Cords—Get them out of the way.

Rugs and shoes—It is challenging to eliminate the lovely little rugs you've collected over a lifetime. And it is tempting at least to keep the one rug inside your entry, which minimizes dirt coming into the house. Removing shoes also minimizes dirt coming inside. But unless you've got good, supportive, non-slip indoor footwear right inside the door for you AND your guests, it's an invitation to falling if you demand that folks go around in their socks. While in some cultures, such as Islam and Japan, it is customary to remove shoes before entering a home, other cultures consider it clearly rude to demand that guests remove their thoughtfully-chosen

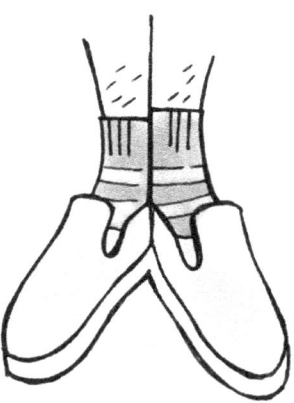

footwear. You might create a more welcoming entrance that minimizes the arrival of dirt. For example, install a metal grill over a recessed area immediately outside of the front door. This reminds folks to wipe their feet and dirt falls away.

Kitchens are also dangerous. Ovens, microwaves,

coffee makers, etc. are all safer and easier to use at waist or eye level. Lighting should include task lighting for areas such as the stove and sink.

Stoves and ovens can be modified to turn off after a specified time or temperature limit. Most irons already have this useful feature.

Heavy pots and pans can be stored at waist level and many pullout systems now exist, making storage easier to view and use.

Do your sinks have two separate hot and cold faucets? A **single-lever faucet** that can be operated with your elbow or a closed fist is enormously helpful.

Again, levers not knobs: if you can use a closed fist or an elbow to open a door, then it's much easier.

Don't forget carbon monoxide detectors and smoke alarms, and put fire extinguishers and baking soda to extinguish fires handy to the stove.

Railings—I'm ranting and railing that we must *always* have railings, even if it is only *one* step or a slippery outdoor walkway.

Upstairs downstairs

Newly-created communities with freestanding homes often offer amenities such as green construction, shared gardens, and walking paths to shopping. What they often *don't* offer is an accessible master bath and bedroom on the main floor. Developers care most about the bottom line and land costs mean that new homes are often two stories. If the home is set up so one is not *required* to go upstairs, the design can be lifelong. The upstairs becomes a guest room or office for the more mobile partner. We are finally seeing houses, condos, and apartments with an accessible master bath and bedroom on the main floor. This is enlightened design.

Another brilliant option for a new two-story home is stacking closets. That makes retrofitting a residential elevator much easier—and cheaper! You lose two closets, one upstairs and one below it downstairs, but you economically gain safe mobility and increase your possibilities of staying in your home forever.

Keeping up with UD

Even people who think they 'get' universal design are often uninformed about new developments, new products, current research and local advocates. There is so much happening!

While products and websites constantly change, the principles of these concepts of user-friendly devices stay the same. If you are having difficulty with whatever device or task, find the solution. If you are not web savvy, your local librarian is. Libraries are no longer just about books—they are technology hubs and every community has one.

Join a group that focuses on Universal Design. Often it's under aegis of the county Division on Aging, a senior center, a group of architects, or realtors, or people with disabilities.

Google Universal Design (UD) often. It's amazing how quickly the field changes. North Carolina State was once the hotbed of UD, but the department no longer exists. It is still challenging to make the concept of UD integral to learning and to planning. It's not sexy enough. Universities also have a huge challenge getting students to study aging and disability. It's also not sexy.

Avoid the technology scams and scallywags

It's challenging but crucial to implement safety with technology. There are numerous pitfalls with scams and scallywags. Therefore, you must set up spam filters, recognize phishing, and don't respond to anything that promises easy money or wants *any* personal information. It is a scam. There is no such thing as easy money.

Learn to use the technology that young people take for granted and some older people resist. I love Siri and Alexa. If you haven't met them, set up a date! Master Google. Bond with your grandkids with Facetime and Zoom. Meet and appreciate your local information librarian—teaching tech is much of what they do. Also, high school and middle schools often have programs in conjunction with a senior center or library on how to use a new device, app, or software.

Learn how to put the people with whom you want to communicate in your contacts. If a caller is not in your contacts, don't answer the phone call. When strangers call and you don't answer, they can leave a voice mail. If they don't, be suspicious and don't call back. If there is a voice mail, you can listen more than once and judge whether or not it might be a scam. Always suspect that it really is a scam. If something seems too good to be true, it is. And if these robocalls are not responded to, eventually you get off the list. I hope.

Again, *never* click on an email link unless you are absolutely sure of the sender. Never click on an email link that might want bank, personal, or financial information. If, for example, Xfinity says your account is closing or needs updating, don't click the link. It's likely to be phishing—fraudulent emails which lure you into clicking a link, giving private information, or revealing a password. If it reads, for example, that you need to contact them to save your email address, credit card, Comcast account or other, assume it is a trap. Go to the relevant website through your browser (Safari, Outlook or other), instead. Then if new information is actually needed, you can provide it. Use two-step verification. For example, have a good password, but in addition, with a two-step process, they then text your phone and give a one-time code. That means that unless someone has your phone and password for it, you are secure.

Never give out your social security number, credit card information, address, date of birth, or *anything* over the phone. If feasible, shop in person, bank in person, and use the web very cautiously. Yet the web is a marvelous tool for everything from home-delivered groceries to fund-raising for non-profits. Supplies would have been very hard to safely obtain during the pandemic without Amazon (yes, I do have stock) and other providers.

Your local library will help you decide what is a scam and what is not and help you with tech support. Although some older people are not tech savvy—librarians are. COVID vaccinations were often only easily accessible through websites, not phone calls. Your librarian can help you directly or direct you to who can.

Email, Zoom, and Facebook bring friends and families together. Again, be sure to limit your Facebook contacts to trusted friends and family and never click a link in an email asking for information or wanting you to click a link even if it uses the name of someone you know. Examine the actual email address. Report scams and spam. Most banks have an abuse email address to which you can forward suspicious phishing.

Establish a face-to-face relationship with your bankers. Often if you are sorting out a problem such as an unlikely charge on your credit card, when the banker calls to inquire about it to the scam or fraud protection department, he or she is asked "Is this person known to you?" You want to be known to the people at your bank. It's an extra advantage in a walkable community that you can walk right in and talk to a real person.

Some of the worst designed devices are those we use every day. Is your phone easy to use and to read? Is it easy to understand voices of callers? Not only do phones continue to get more flexible and useful, they also get more complicated. A tiny keyboard and tinny sound challenge the older user. Higher contrast, larger print, louder audio, enables everyone to use the phone more easily. One model is the Jitterbug *(lively.com)*.

The same goes for entertainment centers, microwaves, thermostats and more.

Aging in place help

If you decide to make your home or apartment friendlier for aging in place, how much will it cost and who will help you do to do the work? Additionally, if you choose to move, there are typically a large number of major and minor upgrades required to prepare a house for the market.

Even the most capable do-it-yourselfer slows down with age. Protect your back by not doing it all yourself and protect your budget by being extremely selective. Happily, there are many resources via your keyboard. If you are not a fan of computers, your local library can help you conduct an electronic search.

I recommend trying to find an "Aging in Place Specialist." In my small community, when I went to the *Certified Aging in Place Specialist* site of the National Association of Homebuilders, more than 30 local companies popped up, mostly architects and contractors.

Of course, some were not what I was looking for, such as a reverse mortgage advocate. At the present time, reverse mortgages need to be considered very carefully. Also listed were some individuals with a poor reputation in my community. Others listed had no information at all.

Select three contractors and obtain at least three references for each. This means a minimum of nine phone calls or emails, but that's cheaper than a botched job or an overpriced remodel.

I would also look up the Northwest Universal Design Council website for ideas *(environmentsforall.org)*. Their home checklist is particularly useful and applies to any area. Other urban centers probably also have similar organizations.

I suggest that any person you hire be licensed, insured, and bonded. While we have had some luck with *sub rosa* (under the table) handypersons, those who operate without credentials, we have also had some bad luck. *Caveat emptor*—buyer beware!

The same goes for plumbers and electricians, although you may not have the leisure in a time of need to get numerous referrals and recommendations. Learn a bit about plumbing yourself. Anyone can plunge a toilet if he or she knows how. Numerous cost-effective self-help methods, such as unclogging your dishwasher with vinegar and baking soda, are easy to do.

Get help at home before you need it

Another service that I recommend is having a housecleaner well in advance of when it becomes a necessity, if you can possibly afford it. When I had unexpected hip replacement, I was so relieved to have a trusted, competent, and even beloved person to do the essential cleaning.

Many women think it self-indulgent to have a cleaner or are convinced that someone else wouldn't do nearly as good a job as they do themselves. First of all, I consider it an equity issue. Some spouses, it appears to me, have never scrubbed a bathroom. Why should I be the only one who cleans the commode?

But more important, as we age, there will be certain tasks that are too difficult or too risky for a frail older person. I found myself standing on a ladder changing a tricky lightbulb weeks after hip replacement. Dumb!

Hiring a helper in advance of necessity precludes hiring a person you don't know in a time of great stress and great need, such as when you are in the hospital about to be discharged. It also precludes dusting that top shelf, falling, and ending up *in* the hospital. Even with a prudent lifestyle, admit it in advance that there may well be a time when you are hospitalized and then discharged and will need help at home.

Hiring helpers is hard. Do you go through an agency that has theoretically screened, trained, bonded, and licensed a housekeeper, handyman, or caregiver? Do you consult a care manager who can advise you about different resources? Did you even know there *are* professional care managers? They can be literally lifesavers if you face a major challenge. Having a care manager when you or a family member is hospitalized can be immensely useful. A care manager is especially important if you are living alone and find yourself so sick you can't care for yourself, but don't want to overstep the kindness of family and neighbors.

A potential resource for locating different services is the Eldercare Locator *(eldercare.acl.gov)*. Keep in mind that it is a huge challenge to maintain such a gigantic database, so listings may be omitted or outdated, but it's a great start.

Some pros and cons

An accessible home with elegant amenities obviously increases its value. While twenty years ago people didn't want to see grab-bars, now they do, especially since there are creative and beautiful options such as *Invisia*. Go ahead—Google it. You'll be thrilled at the elegant hardware that is functional, gorgeous, and, uh-oh, expensive.

Remodeling for aging in place also enables multigenerational housing. The current trend is not in the direction of older people moving in with their kids, but adult children moving in with their parents. Clearly there are upsides and downsides to intergenerational living, but most of the world has been doing it for thousands of years.

All-ages condominiums have some of the advantages and disadvantages of congregate living, but do offer more control. It is your property and while there are reams of rules and regulations, condos are usually run as a democracy, rather than a for-profit industry, like most of retirement housing. Every condo community has its own challenging and changing personality, but they usually offer more social opportunities as well as support services such as landscaping and maintenance.

In any living situation, there will be disagreeable people, to say the least. An interesting book, entitled *The Sociopath Next Door,* proposes a hypothesis that up to four percent of any population is sociopathic. That means in any living situation of more or less one hundred people perhaps four of them might be sociopaths. That doesn't mean they are murders, pedophiles, or rapists. They can be harmless: the hoarder, the obsessive compulsive person, the constant critic. The question is: is he or she a danger to him or herself or others? Unless someone is hoarding dynamite, it's unlikely that an enormous teacup collection or extreme fastidiousness is a problem. In most neighborhoods, everyone knows who the troublesome person is. Your best defense is avoidance, compassion, good manners, and tolerance.

The importance of UD in your neighborhood

Whether you live in a freestanding house, an apartment, a condo, supportive housing, or a manufactured home, your neighborhood is also part of good universal design. I am fortunate indeed that my spouse and I moved to a quiet, sparsely-populated island and live in the central village, near the ferry, the senior center, and the supermarket. Everything is walkable and it is a strong community that is compassionate, engaged, and friendly. I can usually spot tourists, because they don't smile and make eye contact. During the pandemic, masks and distancing were the norm, but even so, eyes smiled and people waved. With 25,000 people, it's not like we know everyone, but we watch out for everyone.

A professor of sustainable transport and director of the Health and Community Design Lab at University of British Columbia, Lawrence Frank, studied satisfaction in different neighborhoods. He found that nearby services that met "recreational and utilitarian needs within a walkable distance," as well as abundant green spaces, created more satisfaction. Of course. Neighborhood stewardship also promotes wellbeing. According to a clinical psychologist at Duke, "By being engaged and active in the community, you're going to feel better," as well as "...making the neighborhood space better...and that's going to make other people feel better."

Another useful concept is "Livable Communities." This also incorporates the principals of ease of use, public transportation, social opportunities and more. According to numerous web sites (and I summarize):

A livable community, and how it differs from a place designed around driving, means the following:
- Freedom of mobility
- A public realm

- The enjoyment of public art and architecture
- Diversity and proximity
- A festive place
- A healthy place
- A place for chance encounters
- Value

This fits well with the World Health Organization (WHO) concept of "Elder-friendly Communities," but I prefer the label "Livable Communities" because they are for all ages. There are many healthy aspects of intergenerational communities.

The Village Concept

It is also possible to create a village in a city. The 'village concept' has been around for decades and is still evolving. Founded in the 80's in Boston, a large co-op community found that residents were aging and not moving. A retired manager organized a non-profit 'village' that organized paid and volunteer services, from plumbing to meal delivery. Members paid a substantial fee to join, as well as monthly fees, but it was so successful that there are numerous sites nationwide. The Village to Village Network *(vtvnetwork.org)* helps communities get started.

The bottom line

For me, the bottom line is not how long an individual lives, it is about quality of life. Bhutan doesn't measure gross national product; that enlightened country tracks gross national happiness. How can this be measured?

The broad categories include psychological well-being, health, time use, education, culture, good governance, community vitality, ecology and living standards. High quality of life and happiness are two different variables, but most would agree that they are related, hard to measure, and important.

The recent pandemic created new areas with crystal-clean air and sparkling water that have been polluted for decades. What few residents who remained in Venice were exclaiming that they could see healthy fish and even dolphins in the canals, a sight not seen for many years. Satellite imagery showed cities in China with far cleaner air than even two months previous.

Humans of all ages also thrive with gardens and decks, easy access to outdoors, nature. Studies show that people heal faster in hospitals if they can see nearby trees. We *all* do better if we can be in contact with nature. A walk in the woods is good for the psyche, the soul, and mental health.

Now that you have improved your understanding of fostering living and aging in place, it's crucial that you understand the importance of knowing, discussing, documenting, and updating your end-of-life preferences. It's much more complicated than it used to be and that's a good thing because you have more choices.

2

Too often a book about aging ends with the chapter on end-of-life issues. By then it may be too late. So, this is

Death with Dignity, or Not—Many Choices

I profoundly appreciate that for most of these issues there is no absolute right or wrong. Knowing, understanding, documenting, and disseminating your choices and the choices of your family and close friends are the crucial components.

When doing my Ph.D. research on long-term care, I interviewed hundreds of people in dozens of nursing homes. Very few of those people wanted to be there, or perceived a desirable quality of life, according to the measurements I was using. Many of them would not have endured the extensive and painful treatments if they had known what life would be like after surviving whatever invasive procedures got them to the hospital and then to the nursing home, such as heart surgery, cancer treatment, or CPR.

Good documentation, well disseminated and understood, often precludes unwanted invasive procedures when a person is older and frail. Sometimes those procedures result in spending the remainder of one's days in a nursing home, which may not be your preference. One has a right to the dignity of living, without someone pounding on your chest, sticking tubes in you, and managing pain to the point of unconsciousness. One has a right not to end one's days in a shared room with a total stranger, underpaid, undertrained, under-respected caregivers, and bad food. You *also* have the right to demand all possible life-sustaining treatments. These are *choices*.

I'm going to quote Ashton Applewhite, brilliant anti-ageism activist, for her take on this difficult subject. She's writing in April 2020, during the pandemic, when many of us are pondering our wills. If you haven't read her book or seen her website *(www.thischairrocks.com)*, this is a great time to do so. She thoughtfully points out, "It's way better to do this stuff around the kitchen table than during a crisis. Hopefully these documents won't come in handy for many more years. But in the weeks immediately ahead, especially for those of us in the pandemic's global epicenter, there are unlikely to be enough medical resources to go around, which has engendered much debate about the value of older people's lives. At any age and in any condition, **everyone has the right to want to stay alive**. Now's the time to make your wishes known and enforceable."

Applewhite adds, "I'd like to know more about the choices available to people who simply cannot take care of themselves any longer." Options in this situation are costly, hard-to-find, and risky—for example, being in a nursing home. In the pandemic, nursing homes experienced the highest death rate, a total of 40% in

2020, for both residents and for staff—higher than in any other situation!

In some cases, I recommend dying. I'm not making a dark joke. For many elderly people who are at the point where they 'simply cannot take care of themselves,' without invasive procedures such as intubation, or risky and expensive institutionalization, some people would prefer a natural death, ideally with pain management and hospice care. Although it's uncomfortable for families and friends to discuss, the conversations on end-of-life choices are essential. For example, with limited respirators, if my choice was between saving myself or saving a teenager, intubate the teenager. Besides the probability of full recovery for people in their 70s (not good) versus teenagers (good), I would step aside for a person who could go on to have decades more of life.

Time to talk about end-of-life

I had the experience of sitting in on a University of Washington ethics committee discussing end-of-life. I was working as director of the office of retired facility and staff, many of them quite old. The speaker, a physician, looked around at the two dozen people there and said, "I can tell just by looking at you right now who is likely to die in the next year." Most of the attendees looked shocked, but the three or so other MDs present nodded in agreement.

While we can't know exactly when someone will die, most physicians can easily answer the question, "Would it surprise you if this person died in the next year?" For those physicians who would not be surprised, it is time to help that patient start talking to hospice. Far too often, the doctor does not. Only recently have medical schools started teaching about end-of-life treatment and care. For many years, it has been taboo. Those studying to be doctors were untrained in the conversation and the realities.

Many physicians don't like the idea of telling people they are 'ready' for hospice. Death is difficult to predict. Not only that, but the arbitrary six-month rule in the U.S. was created to limit the cost of hospice, which, when started in Britain after WWII, was intended for the last *year* or more of life. U.S. insurers, as well as Medicare and Medicaid, thought it would be too costly and came up with six months. In fact, hospice, rather than being more costly, is frequently more cost efficient. Many studies suggest that those on hospice care incur less expense in the last year of life than those who are not on hospice. A recent study, *(pubmed.ncbi.nlm.nih. gov)* found that if, upon entering the emergency room, patients who met specific criteria were given palliative care consults, on average there were significantly shorter stays and significantly lower cost.

Palliative care and hospice

Palliative care and hospice differ. Both provide comfort. However, palliative care can begin at diagnosis and be part of treatment. Palliative care is not time-limited. Hospice begins when treatment is considered to be futile and the person is not going to survive.

Hospice is a team approach for end-of-life care. Hospice nurses and physicians are experts at pain management, and the doctors, nurses, social workers, volunteers, chaplains, and aides work together to provide the best possible quality of life without imposing life-continuing treatments such as chemotherapy, surgery, radiation, etc. It is usually known as comfort care. Treatments such as radiation are used if the objective is to reduce pain. Hospice can take place in *any* setting, including at home, in a nursing home, in a hospital—anywhere. Both for-profit and non-profit agencies, as well as various religious organizations, provide hospice.

The Centers for Medicare & Medicaid Services, *(www.cms.gov)* and the Code of Federal Regulations *(www.ecfr.gov)* very specifically define hospice. Each state issues licenses for hospices under similar regulations. An organization must be licensed to provide hospice services. Hospitals have been known to say, "We provide hospice care," when they are not licensed hospice providers.

Do go gentle into that good night

Poet Dylan Thomas wanted his father to fight against dying. Of course we do not want the people we love to die. But I believe that we not only want to avoid premature death, but also pain and prolonged suffering, both for ourselves and for the people we care about.

What is premature? I don't know. Past the average life expectancy? No; I would say a mature death is one that is not unexpected. It is on time. It will be different for every individual.

What is unnecessary suffering? Again, this is highly individual. But, for myself, I can state that, other than for a short period of time, if I cannot breathe, eat, and process nutrition on my own, I do not want to be intubated. I do not want artificial nutrition and hydration for more than a few days. I do not want dialysis. I do not want pain.

Also, it is much more difficult to cease invasive measures once they are started than it is to refuse them initially. Even non-invasive measures can be life-prolonging, even though prolonging life may not be wanted.

If I can no longer recognize my family, cannot feed myself, and have no hope of recovery, such as with advanced dementia, please do not feed me. As a hospice volunteer, I saw dozens of people with end-stage Alzheimer's, who could not speak, did not recognize the people they loved, and could not feed themselves. They were spoon-fed food they had not selected. They had little sense of hunger or thirst. But if you stuck a spoon of pureed meatloaf in front of his or her mouth, it would be consumed automatically. Watching one aide in a nursing home spoon-feeding a resident on hospice, I suggested that it was an example of stimulus-response. She looked at me uncomprehendingly and asked, "What's stimulus-response?" She had no science background to actually understand what was happening.

Many studies have found that introducing food and liquid into someone who is in the latter stages of dying, either by hand or by tube, causes physical suffering. The body is shutting down, and processing food and liquid is painful.

For myself, I do not want to burden the health care system with exorbitant costs to prolong my existence at end-of-life. I would prefer that money to be spent on prenatal care, patient education or disease prevention.

"We've taken care of that."

Over and over I hear well-informed individuals say, "We've taken care of that. Our health-care providers have our end-of-life documentation." Do you realistically think anyone is going to look those up when you show up unconscious in the emergency room, even if the ER is within your health-care provider's facilities? I suggest that they may not. How likely is it that your designated decision makers will have the documentation with them and even in a situation in which they know and understand your preferences, there will be too many unknown variables to make a perfect decision. For example, you may have specified that you want full treatment "if there is a good chance of full recovery." The medical professionals in the room will not be able to predict that.

Often, adult children think that the situation is well taken care of because mom has the brightly-colored "Physician Orders for Life-Sustaining Treatment" (POLST) posted on the door or fridge (more on that later). Do you think that the emergency personnel who responded to the 911 call will postpone cardiopulmonary resuscitation (CPR) while they check the document? Yes, they are required to check for DNR. If you do want "full code"—all possible treatment—then you need a POLST. But more on this later in this chapter, so keep reading.

Four important documents required

I assume that while many people reading this book are older adults, they are not likely to die within one or two years. Even so, at the very least you need *four* important documents, not just two. I also strongly recommend also having both a Values Statement and an Alzheimer's Disease/Dementia Mental Health Advance Directive in addition to your living will documents. All documents should be widely distributed.

Durable Power of Attorney for Health Care: Who can make decisions for you if you are medically unable.

Medical Directive: What you want under what circumstances

Values statements: Under what circumstances would you consider living or dying. *(endoflifewa.org)*

Alzheimer's Disease/Dementia Mental Health Directive: To be created while you are *compos mentis*, legally able to make decisions. *(endoflifewa.org)*

Most people assume that if they have created their Durable Power of Attorney for Health Care and their Directive to Physicians, they have completed their paperwork. But no! However, you do absolutely need those, and they need to be updated within at least the past five years.

Those two forms are easily available online on websites such as End of Life Washington, AARP, and others.

There are also many other useful forms for these documents. If these links don't work, because the web changes all the time, search for End of Life Washington, AARP, or Living Will Forms. There are numerous legal forms which are free.

Copies of these documents should be with your lawyer, your family members, your immediate neighbors, your health care providers, your closest friends, and anyone else who may be likely to be with you in a life-threatening medical situation. You may even want to carry copies with you.

Be sure to have a "Plan B" designated decision-maker. I have a younger couple living nearby for my durable power of attorney for medical care, and if either of them is unavailable at the time, then there is a local geriatric care manager. I figure at least one out of three will be around.

However, I do *not* recommend "Five Wishes." If used as is, it precludes Death with Dignity, an important option for many. By *precluding*, I mean that a person who has signed the Five Wishes document, and has, for example, late stage ALS (often called Lou Gehrig's disease), horrifically painful end-stage cancer, or other excruciating terminal disease, cannot use the Death with Dignity law. Five Wishes specifically states that, "I do not want anything done or omitted by my doctors or nurses with the intention of taking my life."

Even with appropriate end-of-life documentation, there are numerous painful stories of these crucial 'living wills' being misinterpreted, disregarded, not easily available, and/or not covering the specific life or death situation.

It really *is* challenging and complicated

Obviously, the process of creating and distributing these documents is painfully challenging and complicated. The reason that it seems so complicated is that it *is* complicated. The reason that it seems so emotionally charged is that it *is* emotional. End-of-life issues are legal, cultural, familial, and personal. Friends and family often hesitate to openly discuss these painful topics. Experts disagree. Your spiritual advisor, therapist, physician, adult children, and spouse likely will all disagree about what is the right action in an end-of-life situation. If you have more than one sibling, they almost always will disagree. If you have grandchildren, I guarantee they will not agree with you. Be very careful about who you designate to enact your desires at the end of life.

It is no wonder many folks wait until it is too late to get this crucial task completed.

When is too late? You might consider that when you are of legal age, 18, it is time to document your preferences. Teenagers experience disasters more than many, except the very old: car wrecks, football head injuries, cancer, suicide attempts, and more. It is, however, admittedly unlikely that anyone under 60 will create their end-of-life documentation. Once we hit 60, the statistical probability of death grows greater every year.

A baby boomer—those born between the years of 1946 to 1964—can expect to die at an average age of about 85. However, that is the average. This means that half will die sooner. There are numerous life expectancy calculators; Social Security has one at *(www.ssa.gov)* and there are many more. It's interesting to add variables such as family health history, alcohol and tobacco use, and weight/height ratio. It is fascinating to learn, for example, how much longer you might live if you are a non-smoking vegetarian versus a carnivorous bon vivant.

The POLST

Many people assume they have done what is needed for themselves or family members if resuscitation is wanted (or not wanted) because that brightly-colored Physician Orders for Life-Sustaining Treatment (POLST) has been created and posted on the fridge of his or her residence, be it private home, assisted living, or a nursing home.

As noted earlier, once 911 is called, EMTs are always going to do CPR unless DNR orders are in the POLST *and* it's easy to find and read, up-to-date, and fulfills legal requirements. Otherwise, they may still perform CPR in spite of the expressed wishes of family and caregivers present. They may not look for the POLST, because it is always crucial to start CPR as soon as possible. If you really do not want resuscitation, I heard one expert say semi-seriously, "Have DNR tattooed on your chest." My lawyer, however, advises me that while this is honored in my county, it is not honored in others!

Who should have a POLST? One answer would be anyone whose physician, when asked the question, "Would you be surprised if this patient died in the next one or two years?" would reply, "No, I would not be surprised." Conversely, if you have a life-limiting chronic condition or an acute illness likely to result in death, you may want to specify that you *do* want CPR, if indeed you want to continue living. Even if the physician deems them futile, you may want to demand all possible interventions if you have unfinished business, are satisfied with your quality of life, or have personal beliefs that dictate your choice.

While most states in the U.S. have POLST forms, it appears that some do not. To find out if your state uses this form, visit *www.everplans.com* (I don't know enough about this organization to recommend or not recommend it, but the list is useful.) The POLST is a legal DNR but it can conversely document the preference for full code, which means, basically, "Do everything possible to prolong life." The POLST also has questions about full treatment, selective treatment, and comfort-focused treatment. Therefore, it's not just a document designed to preclude or encourage resuscitation; it encompasses much more.

What if the person is in a private home and a neighbor or tradesperson happens upon your family member who has gone into cardiac arrest? Is he or she going to look for the POLST on the fridge? Probably not, especially if the dying person is in the yard, at the mailbox, at the senior center, etc. There are small green cards that indicate POLST wishes that can go in a wallet, but what are the chances someone will look there? If you find someone collapsed and not breathing, are you going to go through their wallet and *then* start CPR?

If the person is a resident in assisted living or a nursing home, it can get tricky and messy—as are so many issues at the end of life. A newly hired staff person may chance upon a person on the floor, panic, and call 911. Some facilities forbid staff from lifting a person off the floor and therefore they *must* call 911.

If your family member lives in supported housing (and supportive housing means any setting with caregivers, from nursing homes to care at home,) be sure to thoroughly question the staff, from administrator to caregivers to housekeeper, as to what he or she would do if they walked in on someone who is in cardiac arrest, or even just on the floor unable to get up. Most of them, whether they will admit it or not, will call 911.

Then, are the EMTs going to inspect the fridge when someone is in active cardiac arrest? No. They will use a defibrillator. In fact, just about anywhere an older person at the end of life might be, except hospice, whoever is around is likely to call 911. If 911 is called it means that resuscitation is wanted. Otherwise why would you call 911?

A dear friend and neighbor in her 80s was quite specific that she did not want CPR. She carried her POLST around in her pocket wherever she went and often reminded her companions of her wishes. Indeed, when she went into cardiac arrest, she was quickly surrounded by family and friends who were with her until she died. Exactly what she wanted.

To sum up, usually discussions of end-of-life documentation are: 1) medical power of attorney 2) medical directive, 3) POLST (if DNR); as well as 4) special documented options if one has dementia or wishes to hasten death.

Death with dignity

I taught a course on end-of-life issues for over ten years. Some of the most difficult exchanges were about Death with Dignity laws. Of course, not everyone's philosophy or belief system supports these laws. It is rarely used, and with good reason. But it can be an essential choice to have.

As of this writing, California, Colorado, District of Columbia, Hawaii, Maine, Montana, New Jersey, New Mexico, Oregon, Vermont, and Washington State all have Death with Dignity laws. Ethically, it must be discussed with patients and clients in those states. The National Association of Social Workers' Code of Ethics makes it clear that you need to inform a person of all options, even if you personally disagree. Many other states, such as Massachusetts, are considering the law.

The Washington State Death with Dignity Law, like the other states which have enacted such laws, allows terminally ill adults to request life-ending medication. Patients must be 18 or older, be Washington State residents, have less than 6 months to live, be capable of making an informed decision, and have the ability to self-administer the prescribed medication.

Two physicians must state that the person is terminal; the patient's request must be in writing, witnessed by two people at the time of signing, and also requested orally 15 days apart.

In 2020, in Washington, with a state population of 7.7 million, 340 individuals were dispensed the Death with Dignity medication. 75% had terminal cancer, and 20% had neuro-degenerative disease, including ALS.

Death with Dignity is *not* physician-assisted suicide. The medications must be self-administered and one must be cognitively intact and not depressed. Anyone depressed, suicidal, or mentally compromised does not qualify. Those who appear suicidal or depressed are evaluated and counseled by a mental health professional. If determined to be depressed, suicidal, or cognitively compromised, they are ineligible to use the law.

We very much need to talk about dementia and end-of-life choices with our families, neighbors, health-care providers well ahead of the actual need. Yet, it is painful to initiate such a conversation. It takes courage and determination.

Discussing with family and friends

Until I began teaching the course on end-of-life issues many years ago, I had not done my own documentation. After all, I was in my forties and robustly healthy. But in creating useful homework for my students, I was obligated to do the same homework myself. It consisted of:

- *Writing my own obituary;*
- *Stating funeral and memorial wishes;*
- *Documenting or updating end-of-life wishes, (at that time a Durable Power of Attorney (DPA) for Health Care and a Directive to Physicians); and*
- *A short paper on death traditions in a culture different from my own.*

I found a form I felt was flexible, comprehensive and useful. (There are many better ones now.) I filled it out and made copies for all my family. I also made copies of the blank form for everyone in my family. I took them all and distributed them at Thanksgiving. I am so much fun at parties! My family, while not enthusiastic at the time, was grateful to have her completed form when my mother was diagnosed with a terminal brain tumor. A cruel and crucial reality is that you must complete these forms while you are *compos mentis*, of sound mind.

Voluntary Stopping Eating and Drinking (VSED)

Another option, perhaps less daunting legally, but possibly more difficult personally, is Voluntary Stopping Eating and Drinking (VSED). VSED is a legal, ethical, and effective way to achieve a peaceful death. According to End of Life Washington, a study of hospice nurses gave VSED an 8 out of 10 scoring, or better, than Death with Dignity (DWD) in terms of suffering, pain, and peacefulness (Ganzini, 2003) *(endoflifewa.org).*

A revered university professor and founder of Group Health, now Kaiser, Charles Riddell Strother died as he lived, an advocate for the right to die with dignity. According to his January 6, 1998 obituary in the *Seattle Times,* Dr. Strother was "A staunch supporter of the right of patients to refuse nutrition and drink." After seven days of abstention, he died at 90 as he wanted to—in his own home surrounded by family and friends and without pain. His daughter wrote about the experience with pride. Because of his age and disabilities, Dr. Strother was no longer able to be an advocate for the social issues he cared about. A close friend, Aubrey Davis, said, "He was a very complete person," and his death was consistent with his views.

Death is expensive

When I was the director of the UW office of the retired faculty and staff, a distraught young woman called to ask about her recently deceased mother's retirement benefits. Sadly, it was not the type of retirement income that the person of a deceased family member would inherit. It was clear that the daughter was struggling financially. She had put her mother's expensive funeral and burial on a high-interest credit card and was unable to make the payments. If she had called before she charged the expenses, a university fund would have provided advice and even money to help mitigate the cost. Now it was too late.

Two essential organizations to learn about are People's Memorial Association *(peoplesmemorial.org)* and the Funeral Consumers Alliance *(funerals.org)*. These nonprofit organizations monitor death expenses nationally. There is a huge range to such expenses. For example, cremation prices can vary by as much as 750%. The average cost for direct cremation, which uses heat and flame to reduce the body to bone fragments, is $1484, and ranges from $490 to $4,165 in Washington State. Burials range from $698 to $4,791. Less than half of U.S. funeral homes post their prices on line and some even require that you get prices from them in person.

People's Memorial is a co-operative founded in 1939 and requires a one-time membership of $50. This Washington State website will direct you to a similar organizations in other states *(peoplesmemorial.org)*.

Grief can bring out deep, difficult emotions and sometimes spending money on a memorial is a relief. A person might start a go-fund-me page, regardless of whether the money is needed or not, or donate in memory to a non-profit that the deceased person supported. Diverse cultures all over the world often have lavish funeral ceremonies, costing even more than weddings or major holidays. Spending money may be therapeutic for some.

Cemeteries are notoriously costly, and have salespeople skilled in persuading people to buy burial plots in advance, "To ease the process of death for your loved ones by pre-paying." *Caveat emptor*, buyer beware! These are lucrative chunks of real estate. Not only that, but they require costly cement-lined holes, so that as the coffin ages and collapses, there is still a smooth lawn. The same is true of trees, statuary, etc. The cemetery's ideal is to have an easy-to-mow lawn. Lawns are environmental disaster areas that require polluting fertilizers and herbicide, as well as gas-guzzling machines with high carbon emissions. In addition, lawns do nothing to mitigate global warming. Cremation also has a high 'carbon footprint.' What then might be the most environmentally thoughtful way to deal with remains?

Personally, I'd like a green or natural burial, where I can simply be composted in a natural setting. Such options are now easier to find with a web search. I just learned about the latest green way to go, so to speak. It is called 'Natural Organic Reduction.' Washington State is the first to make it legal and it is offered through People's Memorial. Basically, the body is processed in an enclosed container with organic matter such as wood chips, alfalfa, and straw. Over about a month, the microbes turn it all into about a cubic meter of soil. I've put this in my burial directive. New green options continue to become available, so you may want to research current possibilities.

Some thoughts on making a will

Don't forget to designate who will take your pets. Beloved dogs and cats sometimes end up at the pound when there are no plans for succession.

Besides indicating who gets the dog, the money

and the valuables, you might consider how your personal history and the history of those you love can be preserved, if that is important to you. Family art, antiques, photos and correspondence might be treasured differently by different people.

History museums might value historic artifacts, old documents, maps, and photos. Our "Friends of the Library" has experts who triage all donated books to sift for those of value to collectors, those that will sell in their book sales, and those that should be recycled by being 'pulped.' Many thrift stores also sell books. I remember how horrified I was to find popular paperbacks in our condo paper recycling. Those, one way or another, should be available to those who would like to read them. At the very least, they can be put in a 'freecycle' area.

As one ages into being 'an older person,' I suggest giving family heirlooms to younger family members in the present time. Why wait until you're dead for them to enjoy your stuff? Your grandchildren may deeply enjoy your jewelry, your vintage clothes, your most elegant scarves you rarely wear.

In my boomer cohort, many women lament that their adult children don't want their china or silver. It is a sadness to some, but a reality that life is more casual now, and many of us celebrate festive meals, not with fancy table settings, but with fresh flowers and homemade treats. Nevertheless, there is often a new interest in a beloved family members' possessions after they have died.

And there is typically a great deal of interest in the will after a family member has died.

3

The F Word

Getting your $$$$ together

There was a dirty word in my family that we were not supposed to say. The "F" word. It was not to be talked about in 'nice' circles. When I presented the "7 Actions to Take" (to stay out of a nursing home) to graduate students in social work, they would often get six of the actions but not the F word. What would you guess is the F word? *Finances.*

Soon enough most older people come up against this cruel fact: you will have a more independent old age, over which you have more control and choices, if you have money. You can, for example, modify your home. You can purchase services and health care. You can pay for entertainment and exercise opportunities.

Rich people rarely end up in nursing homes—poor people do. Doctors don't usually end up in nursing homes, but nursing aides do. Lawyers don't often live in nursing homes, but their secretaries do. Professors rarely end their days in nursing homes, but their administrative assistants might.

Those entering a nursing home may start out with plenty of money, but it would take little over a year to burn through a $100,000 nest egg at the U.S. average of rate of $7513 per month (2021) to pay for a nursing home.

People with dementia, even advanced Alzheimer's, do not require institutional care, if there are funds, friends, family, and paid caregivers to help, as well as a disability-friendly place to live. Cognitive impairment is a disability, and much of what is described in the previous chapter on Universal Design is dementia-friendly.

Some couples think of their home as their 'long-term care insurance policy'. This leaves a great burden on the surviving spouse, who may outlive the deceased spouse by many years and may not be able to pay for needed care.

It is crucial to understand the difference between Medic*aid* and Medi*care*. The latter only provides for a limited nursing home stay for rehabilitation. Be sure that you or the person you love spends three nights in a hospital prior to recovering in a rehabilitation facility, because otherwise it may not be covered by Medicare. For example, hip replacement often only requires an overnight hospital stay. But if you need help and your spouse cannot bathe or toilet you, you may need to hire someone out-of-pocket. The nursing home rehab might have been covered by Medicare had it followed a three-day hospital stay.

Medicaid is the federally- and state-funded program for those who are medically indigent, which is stringently defined in terms of income and disability. You must 'spend-down' to poverty levels to qualify. About 65% of nursing home residents are funded by Medicaid.

Find your regional insurance advisors through your state's health insurance assistants program, *(seniorsresourceguide.com)*. These trained advisors are free and not selling anything, just giving away good advice.

Check up on "eldercare attorneys." When I looked up several in a referral website, a number of them claimed to be eldercare specialty lawyers but did not necessarily have the training to do other than help with wills, a lucrative specialty. However, wills are not the same as planning for long-term care and end-of-life preferences. Clearly, wills are for after you die. Long-term care planning is about understanding and financing what might happen before you die.

Also, be thoughtful about long-term care insurance. It is a logical premise that one should be able to insure for an expensive risk. However, long-term care insurance is costly and hard to access. There are gatekeepers, by which I mean a social worker or RN who assesses your "5 activities of daily living" and decides whether or not your insurance will pay for help for long-term care. I like to use the DEATH acronym because it is memorable:

Dressing

Eating

Ambulating

Toileting and

Hygiene

In other words, if you cannot perform these activities and have no one to help you, you will die prematurely. However, these are difficult to measure and often arbitrary. For example, if you have severe arthritis, you may not be able to dress independently first thing in the morning. However, if you shrug into your bathrobe, shuffle into your slippers, and get to the kitchen for some food and caffeine, you are able to dress by yourself an hour later.

Usually, your long-term care insurance will not kick in until you are severely disabled and of course there are co-pays, deductibles, etc. It may be better to put aside money in a safe investment that you can access when needed. Since it is optional and costly, most people do not buy long-term care insurance, and thus you are not sharing the risk with a large population. Car insurance is more affordable because it is mandatory. The payouts are financed by many people.

Sometimes the only reason a person is in a nursing home is because of dementia, which usually lasts many years. Especially if the person is combative, family members cannot or do not want to take care of him or her. As already noted, with sufficient funding and a trustworthy administrator, people with dementia can stay at home happily even until hospice is needed. Since short-term memory fails first, and long-term memory stays in intact, possibly for a decade or more, a familiar environment is enabling.

And, as we've already discussed in Chapter 2, having specific end-of-life care decisions documented can preclude nursing home care. Personally, if I don't recognize immediate family members, don't feed me; don't treat me with antibiotics if I get pneumonia. Just let me go. This may sound cruel, but is it any crueler to coax a person to suck spoonfuls of pureed meatloaf from an aide in a nursing home? If that person can no longer speak or toilet independently, or recognize beloved family members, I personally would not want to continue with that dreadful quality of life, not to mention the quality of life of associated caregivers and family. It is not a decision to make for others, but it is a crucial decision to make for yourself and thoroughly document while you are still competent. Make certain that you have designated and available advocates to be durable powers of attorney for health and finances. It is also important to note that when a person is nearing the end of life, introducing food and hydration causes pain and suffering. The body is shutting down and cannot process food and drink.

A persistent myth about Americans is that we don't care for our disabled elderly family members. The reality is that a huge amount of care is provided by family members, a majority of whom are female. The statistics are hard to compile. So much depends on how you define caregiver. Is it an adult daughter who comes every day with groceries and spends hours doing cleaning and laundry? Is it a neighbor who checks in daily? Is it a paid worker financed by the family who comes every other day? Is it the daughter with whom demented dad is living? Is it the dutiful daughter who visits mom twice weekly in assisted living? Depending on definition, probably every person with a family will be, has been, or is involved as a caregiver. Even more people will be involved in the future, as boomers age. It is horrifically difficult, uncompensated, unglorified, unglamorous work. It is stressful, physically and emotionally challenging, and often rewarding as well.

Many older people have no living nuclear family or family members are widely dispersed geographically. Sometimes friends or caregivers wonder "why doesn't the son or daughter (or whoever) come more often?" Perhaps it is an adult child who was abused by the parent in the past. Perhaps it is an alcoholic son who is abusive to the parent. Every family has dysfunction—it is a question of degree and coping.

Having financial control and good oversight and management can enable an elder, even a significantly compromised elder—to remain in the living situation that he or she prefers. Honoring personal preferences, even of severely compromised older people, contributes substantially to perceived quality of life.

It is even possible that someone with severe disabilities would prefer a nursing home, particularly if able to choose it from a variety of options. I interviewed a Navy veteran who, although not terribly disabled, liked the nursing home in which he was living. He found the discipline and routine reassuring. He even like the food! After a lifetime of crowded, institutional living, it was what he was used to.

Unassisted living

Generally speaking, homes are many older peoples' major financial asset. Deciding to move or to stay, to rent or to own, are decisions fraught with potential for error. The housing market is volatile, unpredictable, and fickle.

A recent article in *The New York Times*, March 16, 2020, examined the pros and cons in an article by Susan B. Garland entitled "How to Solve the Rent-or-Buy Puzzle." *(www.nytimes.com/2020/03/12/business/retirement-rent-buy-home.html)*. One option is to sell the family home, rent a smaller place to live and invest the profit from the sale of the home in a safe fund to live on the rest of one's life. When you consider maintenance, taxes, or inconvenient location, it may pay to rent an accessible home in a walkable neighborhood.

Then came COVID, not to mention Russia's war on Ukraine. Who knows what the real estate market will do? Who knows what even the safest investments will do? It's probably not a bad idea, although a whacky one, to set aside an amount of actual cash and easily liquidated items, whatever those are. It's certainly more logical than hoarding toilet paper!

I realized at an early point in my career of working with older people that it is horrifically easy to outlive your income. Put off starting Social Security to the latest date feasible. Consult with your local Social Security office, preferably in person, to review the criteria and statistics. Your benefits are based on your earnings and date of birth. Your life expectancy is based on multiple variables. If you have a life-limiting illness, go ahead—start Social Security at an early date. If you are fit and active, and if you can possibly forego starting Social Security early, by all means start as late as is actuarially logical. By that I mean, at what point would you make more money, based on your potential benefit and projected life expectancy. The same with your 401ks. Until you reach 72, there is no minimum distribution that you are required to withdraw. Save it if you can.

Money is not my area of expertise. Have trusted financial advisors, free if at all possible. Many employers have advisors for free. Your bank, where you should establish face-to-face relationships, should have a person who can advise you on specific matters. Your investment organizations will often give you trustworthy advice for free, especially over the phone. If you have a reputable friend off whom you can bounce money ideas, do so. Be careful—often family and friends and money do not mix well.

To save or to spend—that is the question

It was hard for me to recognize the importance of money. I was in Volunteers in Service to America (VISTA), Peace Corps, and grad school for years and years of voluntary poverty. And I found it fine. Then, working at Community Services for the Blind in the 80's, I saw how being old and visually impaired did not interfere with a good life. Being old, visually impaired and poor did, especially for women who were single and did not own their own home. When I started a decently paid job at the University of Washington, I figured out how much money I'd need for a down-payment on a house, divided that by 120 (a monthly payment once a month for 10 years), and had the credit union take that out every month. The house I bought 11 years later was a good investment in oh-so-many ways.

Other than begging you to consult multiple experts, I cannot give great financial advice—it is outside my area of expertise. But again I beg you to consult multiple experts. Do not put all your eggs in one financial basket, nor take all your advice from one financial expert. Think about what they do or do not have to gain.

In retrospect, it is wise to forego fancy cars, expensive jewelry, or luxurious vacations most of your life—you'll need that money when you are old. Then again if you scrimped and saved and ultimately find yourself wealthy and 80 years old, you missed the chance for adventurous travel and generous giving. If, as did a savvy professor, you bought a classic Mercedes in the sixties and maintained it meticulously, you could then be using a costly car for reliable transportation for forty years. That's a bargain. There are so many ways to save money and to spend money, that there are no easy answers. But at least ask the questions!

4

Social Support

Family, friends, and government

The 2020-22 pandemic indelibly engraved in our collective psyches the importance of family, friends, and community support. It is intuitive that love, friendship, conversation, even conflict, are essential, but there is so much more that may not seem so obvious. In our later years, a robust social safety net can not only mean the difference between life and death, but positive social support can contribute to a good life *and* a good death.

I am including in this big social support bucket not just relationships but governmental and societal life jackets. We sometimes take programs such as Social Security, Medicare, Medicaid, long-term care, Area Agencies on Aging, non-profits, and public health agencies for granted. Watch out! All of these are often threatened by new administrations, new administrators, and new legislation.

During the COVID crisis, many who were formerly contributors to food banks became recipients. Some agencies make the people they serve feel embarrassed and demeaned. Others do not. So, not only are social services often in jeopardy of negative changes, but services might be provided begrudgingly.

A year into the pandemic, at a time when those in my eligibility tier (70 and over) were struggling to find vaccine appointments, a member of my book group sent an email to all of us, announcing the availability of such appointments at a hospital an hour away. We all successfully signed up. Thank you, Susie! We were among the lucky ones. So many seniors were struggling to get appointments that two local non-profits, whose usual task was to provide volunteers for transportation and other services, trained a cadre of volunteers to find appointments, notify and sign up those eligible, and set up transportation. Thank you, Senior Center and Island Volunteer Caregivers! This combination of personal networks and well-organized non-profits are exemplary and effective.

An American myth

There is a myth in America that, in the 'good old days,' families (read 'women') took care of aging relatives, while now we are selfish and farm out older people to nursing homes. In reality, quite the opposite is true. To reiterate, *less than 5% of all people 65 and older are in a nursing home.* Also, in the good old days, people died much younger. The life expectancy in 1900 was 50 for women and a bit less for men. In 2020, the average person could expect to live to be 80.

Of course, many of those in their 70s, 80s, and 90s need support, and current data suggests that a majority of us will be care givers *and* care receivers at some point in our lives. The interdependence of humans is marvelous and productive. While we are a nation founded on a declaration of independence, in fact at all stages of our lives we give and receive interdependencies. An effort to foster interdependence is a normal and desirable state, even imperative.

A false analogy

The analogy of the equity of babies being dependent on parents and then parents becoming dependent on adult children is false. As they grow from completely dependent infants, humans, in general, will learn to toilet independently, go to school, mature and eventually support families themselves. However, it is unlikely that a disabled 80-year-old will ever get more independent rather than less, despite the wonders of surgery, physical therapy and medications.

Interestingly, the trend appears to be that, while we used to think of elders moving in with adult children, more often today adult children move in with their aging parents. Housing is crushingly expensive, as is homecare. There is social support in togetherness. But don't forget the mantra of many a school of social work, "All families are dysfunctional." To me, it is a question of degree and coping mechanisms.

When you hear a complaint that, "My kids never come to visit," ponder the possibility that this parent might have been abusive, physically or verbally, or both. Not every family is like *Leave it to Beaver*. In fact, sociologist Stephanie Koontz wrote a brilliant book, "*The Way We Never Were*," illuminating with research that blended families have always been the norm, and many families are dysfunctional to the point where that is also normal. She also points out that life expectancy was so low in the past that it was normal to lose a partner to death and then remarry. Divorce was uncommon because women had few rights. But it was normal to have more than one 'life' partner throughout a normal life. She calls it 'serial monogamy,' which sounds like a delicious breakfast to me.

Structured social support

Structured social support consists of two distinct yet intertwined spheres. A nurturing community has both non-profit and for-profit agencies that respect and assist people of all ages, backgrounds, ethnicities, and incomes.

On a human level, we can, individually and collectively, consciously nurture our personal relationships. Think of ways to foster a sense of community in your neighborhood. What comes to mind? Backyard barbecues, joint garage sales, progressive dinners moving from one home to another one, a course at a time, consciously creating connection. In the condo community where I live, we have a weekly social hour.

The pandemic has revealed many lacks in health care in this country, such as an initial shocking shortage of personal protective gear for front-line workers. Many communities responded by sharing skills and materials to sew masks from scratch.

In my small town, the emergency preparedness process set up by our city introduced neighbors to each other and established life-long friendships. Partners in 43 states have used the "Map Your Neighborhood" disaster preparedness program. The website will pop up if you search for "Disaster Services and Supplies." The detailed booklet covers what to do in earthquakes, heat waves, blackouts, tornadoes—the potential disasters list is huge. The official website did not, at the time of this writing, include pandemics, but our city used the structure created by Map Your Neighborhood to recruit leadership, find and share emergency supplies, locate those in greatest need, plan for the future, and alert the community by emails and texts to quickly changing situations.

Elder-friendly communities

A good community is an elder-friendly community.

The World Health Organization (WHO) has created guidelines that transcend countries and cultures. Ireland was the first to be recognized as an elder-friendly country. Montreal, Canada, and Portland, Oregon, are recognized as elder-friendly cities. The free guide to Global Age-friendly Cities, downloadable on the WHO site, lists the following criteria for policies, services, settings and structures (that) support and enable people to age actively:

- *recognizing the wide range of capacities and resources among older people;*
- *anticipating and responding flexibly to ageing-related needs and preferences;*
- *respecting their decisions and lifestyle choices;*
- *protecting those who are most vulnerable; and*
- *promoting their inclusion in and contribution to all areas of community life.*

I would also add that a genuine age-friendly community has a competent Public Health Department, and in my opinion, health insurance for all.

The demented driver dilemma

An important factor in an elder-friendly community is safe, accessible, affordable transportation. Any possible way individuals and communities can provide transportation will foster aging in place. While not all of the oldest-old are unsafe drivers, many are. Yet the lack of public transportation, especially in rural areas, is a huge barrier to giving up a car. In addition, many Americans identify independence with driving.

No one policy has solved the demented driver dilemma. Every family figures out different strategies— or not. We told Dad that the car had been recalled and made sure he had plenty of other options to get where he wanted. Eventually, he stopped asking when the car was coming back. I know some families that have disabled the vehicle. If one doesn't have the mental and financial wherewithal to plan and execute car repair, that's one way to cut down on dangerous drivers.

Not just Alzheimer's, but many of the other dementias—Parkinson's, stroke, Lewy bodies, brain tumors—dramatically reduce the ability to drive. Other age-related disabilities, such as tremors, slowed reactions, stiffness to view side traffic, and more, interfere with driving.

I attended a panel on dangerous drivers at a national aging conference. One organization had created a 'driving advance directive.' The person in peril of being at risk in the future signed a document saying that he or she knew that at some time, "I will be an unsafe driver," and designated a specific person to make the decision as to when the time had come. The audience thought it was a brilliant idea—until someone asked, "Did it work?" "No," was the sad answer.

Most states have a protocol where physicians can report unsafe drivers. One hopes that, when such a report is made, some action is taken. There are even websites, such as Bad Driver *(baddrivers.com)* where you can use your phone to snap a photo of an unsafe driver. This at least creates a record. It isn't clear again whether any action results from being reported. Some state Departments of Licensing have a form that can be used anonymously to request to have unsafe drivers evaluated. As an example, here is the link to the form for Washington state *(www.dol.wa.gov/driverslicense/reportunsafe.html)*.

Many cars now have back-up cameras, as well as sensors around the entire car, warning systems, automatic braking systems and more, to help older drivers (and younger ones too!). Those that can afford it may well benefit from a state-of-the-art car with maximum safety devices. Everyone else on the road will be safer as well.

Teenagers and those over 85 have the highest rate of accidents per miles driven. Getting unsafe drivers out of their cars can save lives, preventing such tragedies as the one that occurred when my 92-year-old neighbor backed over and killed a grandmother in front of her horrified grandchildren. All age groups should be subjected to identical scrutiny. Perhaps we need a comprehensive driving exam for every driver every 10 years?

Affordable, accessible housing

Affordable, accessible housing is another factor that creates an elder-friendly community. Granting permits for new structures can include requirements of a certain percentage being low income and affordable. Ideally, when new multiple-unit housing is designed, local data on what percentage of the population is of various ages and income is consulted. For example, a one-hundred-unit apartment complex could reflect the age of older and/or disabled population and sell at a diverse range of prices. So, if 15%, (a likely figure in the U.S.) is over 70 or disabled, 15% of the units are accessible, including a wheelchair-usable entry and bathroom. How many U.S. communities do this? Few, if any.

An epidemic of loneliness

Some say we are in an epidemic of loneliness exacerbated by COVID. For example a depressing article in *The New York Times* (*www.nytimes.com/ 2022/04/20/nyregion/loneliness*) suggests that the brain detects loneliness "as a threat" and thus releases stress hormones, which can damage health. Such a concept is difficult to measure objectively—because it is so subjective, and few empirical studies have been done. How could one conduct an ethical double-blind, placebo-controlled study? You cannot force research subjects to be lonely. Some people are lonely in a crowd, others are not lonely even when alone.

Fear of death for oneself and for loved ones contributes to pandemic stress, but, while isolation may contribute to a lower disease risk, it may not enhance well-being. What indeed is *perceived* well-being? Social scientists agree that quality of life is important, but there is no agreed-upon good measure of quality of life.

Pets

While tinder, Match.com and other web services make it easier—and riskier—than ever before to date, the unconditional love of a pet can soften the sorrow of loneliness. Dog and cat adoptions soared during the pandemic. And while it is challenging to manage the needs of a dog when working full-time away from home, there is an entire industry of dog-walkers, doggie daycare, and dog-friendly businesses. Also, working from home, as well as pet-friendly workplaces, can enhance quality of life, both for people and for pets. More and more workers are employed in a hybrid job, part in-person and part working from home.

"Zoomers"

Many of us became "Zoomers" during the pandemic and my instinct is that we will continue these electronic meetups even when the COVID epidemic is over. Zoom, or whichever of the programs you use, both free and for a fee, combat not just loneliness and disconnection, but enable us to participate in meetings, conferences, friendships, and family get-togethers that were often inconvenient at best and impossible at worst.

One branch of my dozens of cousins Zooms every Saturday night. One neighbor video chats with her many sisters every Sunday. Our senior center has an 11:30 Zoom every weekday with guest speakers, travelogues, talks on memoir writing, local organizations and more. I Zoom quarterly with a statewide council on invasive plants and animals, which I find fascinating and useful. While I would never drive to our state capital many miles away for such a meeting, I am delighted to virtually sit in on the briefings from all the experts.

Technical devices can aid connecting with family and friends. GrandPad, a tablet specifically designed for seniors, may be worth the large price tag. There are several other devices meant to replace smaller, more complicated phones and larger, more complicated computers. Some libraries and senior centers have devices to lend, so a person can learn if it fills a necessary niche.

Mastering a new device or software can be a cruel diagnostic. If even a very early stage of memory loss is present, a new tool or program can be an exercise in frustration. Listen when someone says, "I don't want to do this." The good old-fashioned landline still works and one can rely on long-term memory to use it well.

Software and devices were used for memorials during the pandemic. It is so important for healing to have some type of ceremony. There is no right or wrong way to do them, but evidence indicates that it is helpful to have a gathering, even if by phone, electronic notebook, or computer.

Home alone for the holidays

The pandemic gave many families the opportunity to reconsider how and why we come together. Zooming replaced flying across the country for holidays. Various relationships appear to have been improved by distance. Skipping Thanksgiving with querulous cousins was a relief! Faking unfelt piety unnecessary. Stressful guilt trips gone. Going forward, holiday gatherings may be more optional than obligatory.

Traditions and rituals can soothe stress or maximize it. Many risked life-threatening infection during COVID to gather with family and religious groups. Consider creating new traditions, such as a solstice celebration, tto fight isolation and promote harmony; celebrations that might be happily anticipated rather than dreaded. Such innovative gatherings of family and friends could have smaller carbon footprints than flying and more space for joy.

Seemingly unimportant social intersections

Other consequential connections are intersections that we may not recognize as vital but help foster a sense of belonging and happiness. They are those seemingly unimportant people with whom you come in contact in a normal day, even during the pandemic. Think of the grocery workers who look you in the eye at your regular market and honestly ask how you are doing (and vice versa). The daily visit from a friendly mail carrier is a little pleasant boost of sociability. Chat with your hairdresser, your physical therapist, your neighbor sweeping her walk. Such seemingly trivial conversations enrich our lives with information, humor, and kindness. In a book entitled *Consequential Strangers,* M. Blau and K. L. Fingerman researched these relationships with people not relations or close friends and found that they help with a basic human need for community.

Negative social support

While it is easy to acknowledge that social support has positive value, we often have a hard time grasping that there is also the opposite—negative support. Think of those people who suck more from you than they return. Not all relationships are symmetrical, nor must they be. But those people who need so much—so much sympathy, so much help, so much listening—can drag you down. At what point is such a relationship harmful to you? How do you weigh the importance of self-interest if you are truly needed?

Consider how much there is that can be sucked from you without damaging the nurturing you give others and that you give to yourself. Of course, relationships in our lives differ greatly and change over time. The same person can be primarily the listener in one relationship and the talker in another. But when it is noticeably unilateral over a long period of time, sometimes self-preservation sets in. Allow yourself, to say, "Sorry, Mom.

I can't come to dinner this week," or, "Forgive me, Angela, I must hang up and take another call." I'm not suggesting totally ghosting family members, except in the case of an abusive relationship, but while blood is redder than water, it's not always the best binding force.

It breaks my heart to have totally one-sided conversations on a regular basis with long-time friends. There are crises in all our lives. At these times, you must receive the pain and sorrow from a dear friend, and listen, listen, listen. However, it can eventually return to a true conversation, in which each person listens and talks. An equal friendship is healthy.

Helping those in grief

One of the hazards of choosing to work professionally with older people is that I repeatedly lose my mentors, my friends, my colleagues. Even worse, as I age, I lose more and more family to death. It is a reality. Losing a pet can also be a painful reminder that life is finite. On the other hand, many years of teaching about end-of-life issues, and personally losing so many of those dear to me, have given me the gift of learning a great deal about what is most helpful to say—and not to say—to those in grief.

When you learn that a person has lost a close friend or family member, particularly a beloved partner, please do not immediately change the subject and describe your saddest loss. This is not about you. Whatever our intentions, it shows an incredible lack of empathy to try to offer sympathy by demanding it in return. There's a famous book on the subject, *Don't Ask for the Dead Man's Golf Clubs.* A young widow with two children was appalled at such comments as, "You are still young enough to remarry." Or, "He's in a better place." To her, a better place was alive by her side.

It is always correct to say, "I'm so sorry for your loss." Or, "I can't possibly imagine how you feel." Because, of course, you cannot imagine how someone else feels, especially with the death of someone much loved. When my beloved husband died, it was agonizing how many people said, "Oh I remember how awful I felt when my husband (wife, father, or whoever) died." It put me in the position of saying, "I'm so sorry your whoever died." While I was sad for their loss, I did not want their added sadness on top of mine at that time.

There is no wrong or right way to grieve and no time limit to 'finish' grieving. Grief takes as long as it takes. I try not to judge a grieving person; each loss is unique and personal. Again, the three most important things you can do are listen, listen, listen. It is a great need of the bereaved to tell their story.

Losses that come unexpectedly, especially death to a younger person, can be especially difficult. It is heartbreaking to lose a parent, but, in most cases, even more tragic for a parent to lose a child. Compounded losses are also more difficult. To lose one beloved family member is horrendously hard. To lose multiple members of your family is crushing. I am thinking of the war in Ukraine as I write.

Dysfunctional grief

Often complicated losses such as sudden or multiple deaths result in dysfunctional grief. What does functional grief look like? Extreme sadness. But *dysfunctional* grief often shows itself as drug or alcohol abuse, family abuse, blank stoicism, fury. I think of the many suicides in the military. The combination of talk therapy and prescription drugs can be effective, and remember that 'talk therapy' is actually a professional listener.

The Native Americans in this country lost countless family and friends, first to diseases to which they had no resistance, then to the so-called "Indian Wars" and forced relocation. They lost their land, their sources of food, their culture, their languages, their religions, and most tragically, their children. All over this country children were taken from their indigenous parents and sent to 'boarding schools' where they were forced to abandon their loved ones, their clothes, even, most cruelly, their languages. Many were physically abused with forced labor and sexual abuse. Experts suggest that these multiple, unresolved, and egregious losses have resulted in manifestations of dysfunctional grieving.

My opinion is that to some extent the demonstrations and some of the destruction that occurred during the pandemic were, in addition to anger at hundreds of years of systemic racism and abuse, also about the losses and resulting grief we were experiencing at that time. We lost our freedom to do normal day-to-day activities, like going to dinner and a movie. Many have lost friends or family to COVID. We appeared to have lost a functioning democracy for a time. Many are grieving the disregard of truth and science. This grief, this anger and fury at injustice and racism, the horrible history of slavery and injustice, were being publicly expressed. There is hope for healing when the depth and profundity of these factors is better understood and addressed.

The paragraph above was written before the shocking destruction at the Capitol Building in Washington D.C., on January 6, 2021. While there is no conscionable explanation of why Donald Trump would encourage people to riot and invade the Capitol Building, I suggest that his followers responded to his mad urging partly because of the grief, stress, and pain of the pandemic. It well might have been, to a certain extent, a manifestation of dysfunctional grief.

Dealing well with loss is immensely helped by positive social support at all levels. Fostering strong positive relationships provides huge benefits for heath, happiness and longevity, which leads to our next chapter.

5

A Bucket of Wellness Factors

Dementia prevention and health

The factors shared in this chapter's bucket are geared to maximize the probability that your last years will be longer, more joyful, and less painful—for you and for the people you love. What you don't know *can* hurt you.

It is only recently that it has been proved that many age-associated deficits are not actually age-related, but lifestyle-related. Doctors used to think that atherosclerosis (hardening of the arteries) was normal aging. But then studies of people in countries such as Japan and Italy, where life is often more active than the U.S., and meat is not typically the main dish, found that many old people have arteries like teenagers.

Similarly, doctors and dentists used to think that osteoporosis was an inevitable part of normal aging. Bones thinned with old age and jaws shrank, and that was that. However, it was learned that not only did bones need vitamin D and calcium, it was weight-bearing exercise that kept bones strong. If someone has osteopenia, the beginning of weak bones, at first it was thought important to protect the person from bone-breaking falls by confining him or her to a wheelchair. The result? It turns out that this causes the bones to thin even more, and walking and balance deteriorate rapidly. Now we recommend physical therapy, guided exercise, increased walking, and weight-bearing exercise.

Exercise

When teaching gerontology, I often told my students that the three most important actions you can take to age well are: 1) exercise, 2) exercise, 3) exercise. Literally, exercise is the most important modification that you can make to improve quantity and quality of life. REALLY! Exercise will help you feel better, look better, sleep better, and be in a better mood. People who exercise have a lower incidence of heart disease, depression, falls, fractures, and perhaps a decreased risk of the demon we all fear—Alzheimer's. There *are* other decisive health interventions with clear benefits. But let us begin with the most important—exercise.

In the not-too-distant past, doctors started recognizing that aging athletes had longer, more disease-free lives. But where was the data? Until relatively late in the 20th century, very little was known about the actual effects of exercise on aging. One theory was that we only had a finite number of energy units (known as ergs in electricity) per lifetime. After a certain age we needed to ration those precious ergs—conserve them so that we could last longer. The idea was manifested in the idea of 'rest homes.' One must 'rest' to save life forces for a longer life. There were no real scientific studies to indicate the contrary until relatively recently.

Scientists, scholars, and philosophers have long pondered what makes a good old age. More and more research indicates that a good old age is a healthy old age. Most of us know intuitively and factually the importance of exercise, nutrition, hydration, sleep, and a passel of other variables that enhance wellness as we grow old.

As far as I can tell, the history of empirical research on aging in the U.S. goes back to about 1940, when a Unit of Aging was established under the National Institute on Heath Division of Chemotherapy, which seems an odd place to start. But the next year, Surgeon General Thomas Parran formed a National Advisory Committee on Gerontology. President Truman convened the First National Conference on Aging in 1950. That doesn't mean the connection between aging well and proactive interventions such as exercise had been researched. Longitudinal studies began in the 50s, notoriously based exclusively on white men, as if women and people of color did not need to be included.

I first learned about research on aging and exercise when I was director of the offices of all retired faculty and staff at the University of Washington, beginning in 1986. Researchers at U.W. Health Sciences piloted a rigorous randomized trial to determine the effects of exercise on aging. They selected the Northshore Senior Center in Bothell, Washington, King County's flagship facility for older people, as the site of the study. For six months, the exercise group took hour-long classes three times a week, consisting of warm-up, cardiopulmonary exercise such as brisk walking or dancing, weights for both arms and legs, and cool down. (Based on various findings, current classes have much the same structure.) The control group—the group not part of the exercise class—received a brochure on protecting the back from injury.

The first interesting result was that more and more people wanted to be in the exercise group. Those folks were having fun, looking good, and fitting into their favorite jeans better! The researchers had to explain scientific research more than once. The control group *had* to stay out of the exercise group until the researchers had more data. The non-exercisers were promised that they ultimately would be allowed to join.

Tests were done quarterly, measuring the times a person could sit then stand in one minute, the exact time it took to get up and go around a cone 100 feet away, and similar measurable activities. The outcome variables were hospitalizations, falls and fractures, depression, and deaths.

As the data accumulated over the years and over multiple sites, it became more and more evident that just three days a week of structured exercise, for an hour each time, significantly lowered the incidence of those unpleasant and unwelcome variables. When I retired from U.W., I took the training and then taught Fitness Enhance classes near my community. I remember when the class I was teaching for the Suquamish Elders no longer needed us to collect data. It was clear that the program worked.

When the results were analyzed and published, the findings were dramatic. As a result, there are now numerous evidence-based senior exercise programs such as Silver Sneakers, Staying Active and Independent for Life (SAIL), Fitness Enhance, and more. Many Medicare supplemental insurance programs will pay all or half of gym membership or class fees.

Exercise and the brain

It is also clear that structured exercise is more beneficial than just plain work like the hard labor required to do construction, landscaping, or other physically taxing jobs. Muscle builds better and injury is less likely in a methodical, research-based program. Physically demanding jobs may even diminish the hippocampus. In a large study conducted jointly by Colorado State University and the University of Illinois,

people who reported regular physical activity on their own time had greater hippocampal volume than people who were inactive during non-work time. People who were in highly physical jobs and did not exercise outside of work had, on average, smaller hippocampal volume. Although much is still not known about this association, it *is* known that the hippocampus plays a major role in learning and memory.

There is other evidence that exercise may help the brain. In a study published in a July 2020 issue of *Science*, researchers at the University of Southern California, among other institutions, found that both young and elderly mice who ran for six weeks performed better on cognitive tests than sedentary mice. A specific liver protein was elevated after exercise, improving brain performance. (There's also an article about the study in *The New York Times*, *How Exercise May Bolster the Brain*, published on July 15, 2020.)

Another *New York Times* article, *(www.nytimes. com/2021/03/03/well/move/exercise-aging-brains)*, specifically examined aerobics and the effects on thinking and remembering in older people. The author, Gretchen Reynolds, asserts in the article, "The idea that physical activity improves brain health is well established." With a sedentary control group, the study cited found that the brain scans of participants in a twice-weekly dance class showed improvement.

Get out however you can

I remember an astute older—and sedentary—engineering professor whose doctor informed him that he was likely to have a heart attack, resulting in death or permanent damage, if he didn't at least start a walking program. Heeding this advice from a fellow scientist, he started by sauntering around Seattle's Green Lake, a flat and attractive 3-mile walk in a park, a couple of times a week. Soon he was circling the lake every other day. On his next visit to the doctor, his blood pressure was down and his cholesterol was improved, not to mention that he looked and felt better. Behavior *can* change and those changes can transform your life.

But just knowing that exercise is good for you isn't

enough to motivate everyone. For me, one inescapable exercise incentive is my dog. The dog and I simply, absolutely, must get outside at least four times a day, and at least a few days a week we walk three or four miles, the popular 10,000 steps. As reported in *The New York Times*, a 2019 meta-analysis of studies (a study of studies) on this subject found that people who own dogs live longer and have a lower incidence of heart disease. For many people (me among them), walking with a dog is one of the inexorable motivators for exercise. In addition, there are the stress-lowering properties of getting outdoors, as well as the proven blood pressure improvements of petting a pet.

A mental health bonus of dog-walking is that, for those who experience Seasonal Affective Disorder (SAD), even spending just 20 to 30 minutes outdoors daily can reduce symptoms such as pervasive sadness, undue fatigue, difficulty concentrating, excessive sleep, loss of interest in normally enjoyed activities, and cravings for starches and sweets.

Clinical SAD was even higher than the normal 5% during the 2020 winter of COVID. Staying mentally healthy is at least as important as staying physically healthy and the two are inextricably intertwined. Those who get regular exercise are happier on the average. Those who are on an even keel mentally are less likely to abuse alcohol, drugs, and fattening foods.

Success suggestions

Walking, to my mind (and to my hips and heart and legs), is the perfect form of exercise. It is free. It can be solitary or companionable. It can be done in all weather.

It can be lazy or cardiovascular. If you don't love it, let's think about what can make it more lovable or, at least, somewhat pleasurable.

Pre-pandemic, I was in three weekly walking groups, two of which, over the years (one of them for two decades), have become support groups of sorts. During the height of the pandemic, two of the groups zoomed weekly. You can find walking groups through your parks department, senior center, community center, or use an app such as Nextdoor. Or start one!

Having a walking buddy with whom you can get together one or more times a week is another successful approach. If we are fortunate, we have friends with whom we enjoy long talks. If you don't have such a friend, this may be a way to nurture such a relationship. Regular rambles can encourage confidences. Although 'friends with benefits' has another meaning today, having a buddy with whom you can confide is crucial to mental and physical health, which (again) of course are inextricably intertwined. Exercising together is the bonus of walking *and* talking.

There are also gifts to walking alone. It can be a meditation in and of itself. Many walkers use devices to listen to music, books, podcasts, and the radio, or just enjoy device-free birdsong. Either way, walking can be a needed chance to be solo, especially if most of your hours are spent in company.

Walking can be done inside on a machine, which makes it easy to check heartrate, speed, and distance. Also, now there are Fitbits, apps on your phone, and other devices that keep a record of activities. In addition, you can listen to books, watch TV, or, if you prefer, enjoy the camaraderie of a gym.

Having an indoor exercise machine in your home is a good solution for some people. I loved it that the Obamas had two side-by-side treadmills so that every morning they would get exercise and crucial couple-time together.

Stress

We often ignore another predictor of good health: stress control. At least as important as diet and exercise factors, doing one can help relieve the other. Any web search of 'alleviating stress' will produce results naming exercise as a stress reducer.

The coronavirus pandemic weighed heavily on most people. Even with the lifting of restrictions as more and more people are vaccinated, COVID continues to be a stressful risk. It has certainly caused many people to become unemployed. A recent study found that people whose income dropped had a corresponding drop in health, and those whose income increased lowered their risk of heart failure, heart attack, or stroke.

Stress affects all aspects of health, from blood sugar and blood pressure, to the immune system. Multiple solutions such as meditation, yoga, and humor can help.

Take care of your mental marbles

Barriers to solutions that we know work for better aging surround us. "I don't have time" is such an easy one to fall back on for many of us. Until the pandemic, many of us were heavily scheduled and not getting in a beneficial number of steps each day. We certainly have fewer demands on our time now. Even a pandemic contains some surprising gifts.

Personally, I revile spherical objects that must be kicked, hit, or tossed. Keeping score means someone loses. I prefer ballet—where everyone is a winner. Then again, ballet isn't that great for a normal body—nor is football. But for many, a competitive sport is a motivator. Pickleball, which originated on Bainbridge Island, near Seattle, is a new national sport—and the state sport of Washington.

Whatever exercise we do, we need to keep in mind the importance of preventing physical brain damage. The brain deserves protection from any and every type of brain trauma, especially but not exclusively, concussions. If you ever played football you are at greater risk for dementia. If you were ever knocked out, your brain suffered, perhaps permanently. Successive insults to the brain are especially damaging. For example, if you get knocked out in a football game and are sent back into play, any second blow to the head risks major brain damage, often showing up years later with premature dementia.

Skiers, sledders, skate boarders, bike riders, surfers, etc., often wear head protection now. If you value your marbles, take care of them!

Another area that can maximize physical health is physical therapy. Again and again, research is demonstrating that professional physical and occupational therapists can improve function, prevent injury, prevent surgery and hospitalizations, maximize independence, and enhance quality of life. And it's often covered by Medicare or your Medicare supplement. Talk with the billing office to learn about insurance and coverage for this life-enhancing health profession that can maintain and improve function. Then stick to the exercises the therapist teaches you every week, forever. Uh-oh—more exercise.

Laugh it off

One way to combat stress is laughter. Laughter may not be the best medicine, but it surely is one of them. Think about what cheers you up. I find that humor is good for lifting my spirits, and watch news, disasters, and dark entertainment sparingly.

In a *New York Times* article from October 1, 2020, Dr. Michael Miller, a cardiologist at the University of Maryland School of Medicine, prescribes humor for health. "Laughter releases nitric oxide, a chemical that relaxes blood vessels, reduces blood pressure and decreases clotting," reports Dr. Miller. Another important finding related to the COVID crisis, is that "...a sense of humor helps people remain resilient in the face of adverse circumstances," according to George Bonanno, a professor of clinical psychology at Columbia University.

A gigantic Norwegian study (53,556 participants!), published in 2016 in *Psychosomatic Medicine*, concluded that the cognitive component of a sense of humor is positively associated with survival of coronary vascular disease in women and with infection-related mortality in men. No explanation is given of the gender difference but, as Mark Twain famously said, "Humanity has one really effective weapon— laughter."

Alan Alda agrees. In an AARP interview in 2020, he voices his belief that the best medicine for humans is laughter. "When you laugh," he says, "you're vulnerable. You're opening yourself up. You're not protected...you let the other person in, and that brings us all closer." When *MASH* aired, despite the laugh track during the rest of the show, the director always omitted it in the surgery scenes, so the doctors could joke around and spontaneously respond to each other.

A senior center member in my community teaches a popular class called "Liberation Laughter." When asked for feedback about the class, a participant wrote: "I want to stress how life-changing your class has been for me. I worry so much less about other people's private opinions and don't bend over backwards, anymore, trying to please them (as if I knew how I could do that). Being silly and spontaneous in front of a group made me realize that I am myself and that I am okay. Period."

Besides laughter, think of other stress reducers you already know. Meditation is a practice that research has proven to be effective. Gardening can be a meditation; spiritual practices are often meditative; walking, hiking, backpacking—all are forms of meditation. Talk therapy with a trusted friend or professional can be stress reductive. I'm sure you can think of more.

Dementia

Dementia is a bucket term for any type of cognitive decline over time. Causes could be head trauma, Parkinson's disease, Alzheimer's, cardiovascular disease, cerebral incidents such as stroke or TIA's, Lewy bodies, prolonged COVID, malnutrition, alcoholism, negative drug interactions, depression, and often a combination of two or more of these. It is currently thought that perhaps 85% of dementias are some stage of Alzheimer's, often in conjunction with other brain damaging conditions.

There is still much to learn. Dementia could be sudden onset, such as a massive stroke, with burst blood vessels in the brain. Often, with rapid treatment, much cognition returns. Other dementias, such as Alzheimer's, start very slowly and gradually with minor short-term memory loss. Perhaps more than a decade later, a serious inability to plan, drive, cook, read, or other activities necessary for living become apparent.

Whether mild cognitive deficits in old age are normal aging or a precursor of dementia is still debated in the research. According to a 2020 talk by Stephen Thielke, M.D., M.S.P.H., from the University of Washington Department of Psychiatry and Behavioral Sciences, "Dementia is a significant chronic loss, in memory, and/or mental functions, involving structural damage to the brain." (You can see the whole talk on YouTube.)

When someone complains, "I have a terrible time finding my keys; I must be getting Alzheimer's," remember that most *teenagers* have trouble keeping track of their keys. Perhaps the person complaining has been misplacing keys since the age of 18. Having useful habits, such as a place for everything and everything in its place, helps a great deal.

The great predictor of Alzheimer's is old age. Approximately one in ten Americans over the age of 65 has Alzheimer's. By the age of 80, it appears to be as much as 30%.

In June of 2020, *The New York Times* published an article, *5 Measures That May Lower Your Alzheimer's Risk*, which focused on the findings of a longitudinal study of 1,845 people, whose average age when it began was 73, and another 920 people, with the average age of 81. After approximately six years, 608 developed Alzheimer's disease. Participants were scored on five behaviors: not smoking, consistent moderate or intense exercise, light to moderate alcohol consumption, a Mediterranean-style diet, and engagement in late-life cognitively challenging activities. "Compared to those with none or one of the healthy lifestyle factors, those with two or three had a reduced risk for Alzheimer dementia, and those with four or five had a 60% reduced risk."

These all involve choices that we get to make about how we live our lives. Because there are obvious benefits, choose:

- *not to smoke,*
- *to exercise regularly,*
- *to drink some, but not much, alcohol* (perhaps— as reported on CNN, a 2021 observational study by Oxford University suggests that there is no "safe" level of drinking as regards the brain),
- *to stay engaged with life, and*
- *to eat a diet rich in fruits, vegetables, fish, and low in meat and processed foods.*

It has long been indicated that those who drink moderately (one glass of wine, one beer, or a single 1.5 oz drink of alcohol a day), on average live longer than teetotalers, or those who drink more than a very low weekly dose. This statement is almost always followed by, "But if you don't drink now, don't start." Of course, it may not be the alcohol. It could be that the type of person who chooses to drink less than five to seven alcoholic beverages a week is the kind of person who eats and exercises thoughtfully, abhors smoking, and engages in productive activities.

Correlation or causality?

Correlation does not establish causality. It could be that healthy living minimizes the risk of Alzheimer's, but it could be that having Alzheimer's means that one chose less healthy options. It may be a chicken and egg situation. Will we ever know which came first?

Current research on dementia almost always shows correlations, which really don't prove anything. For example, a number of studies indicate that people who get, on average, between seven and eight hours of sleep have a lower incidence of Alzheimer's in old age. Is it because sleeping well is good for the brain? Or is it because the degenerative process in the brain inhibits sleep, even in those without symptoms of Alzheimer's but already in the process of brain function loss? Another example: those who exercise three times a week, for at least an hour each time, usually have less symptoms and diagnoses of Alzheimer's. Did exercise protect the brain? Or did Alzheimer's interfere with doing regular exercise? We don't know. We just know that correlations such as

Alzheimer's and sleep, or Alzheimer's and exercise, do not establish causality.

One risk factor we can exclude is family history. What?! Happily, this may be true. Other than early onset Alzheimer's, which is younger than 65, and relatively rare, there does not seem to be a genetic predisposition. So, if you are over 70 and cognitively intact, even if both your father and grandfather had Alzheimer's in their 80s, it is not predictive that you will have the disease. Your forebearers just lived long lives, which is what increases the incidence of Alzheimer's.

Don't want it? Die young.

Brush your teeth!

Until we had dental implants, dentists pulled rotten teeth and fitted us with false ones. Without the stimulation of biting and grinding food with teeth attached, the jawbone shrank. With implants, the bone is stimulated and stays strong and intact. But there are more good reasons to take good care of your teeth and gums.

Controlling for smoking, body mass index, heart disease, education, sex, and age, when compared to people with good oral health, those who had severe gingivitis with tooth loss had a *22% increased relative risk for dementia.*

Other studies indicate that the bacteria present in periodontal disease can travel along the nerve that connects the mucous membranes in our mouth directly to the brain, potentially infecting it. Poor dental health is also a risk factor associated with cardiovascular disease and diabetes, which in turn are more known risk factors for dementia. Now you have more reasons than ever for excellent dental hygiene!

Poor oral health is also correlated with lower education and income. Higher education correlates with less incidence of Alzheimer's. Some good reasons (should you need any) to encourage (and help finance?) your grandchildren to stay in school.

Use your eyes and ears

There appears to be an association between uncorrected hearing and vision loss and a higher risk of Alzheimer's. So, get the best correction you can find and afford. An annual visit to your optometrist can ensure that your eyeglass prescription is optimal, as well as getting a regular check-up for preventable vision loss from eye diseases such as glaucoma.

Recent studies indicate that half the people in the U.S. 75 and older have some level of hearing loss. Hearing loss of course affects quality of life, but it also appears to impact cognition and dementia risk. If information cannot get in, it cannot be retrieved. Children are particularly difficult to understand, and most grandparents absolutely want to communicate with their grandkids.

Why is there more stigma to wearing hearing aids than to wearing glasses? Of course, we all know vain people who only resort to glasses when absolutely required to read. But a much larger percentage of people refuse to get hearings aids. They are costly. They are visible. Both statements are true. But it is also true that they *do* work.

Hearing aid technology has improved, and the

price has gone down. Ten years ago, hearing aids cost more than twice as much and were twice as difficult to use. These days, even Costco has affordable hearing aids comparable to the most expensive models sold in medical clinics. The testing is the same and the audiologists are as well trained. Initial instruction and fine-tuning are required but now you can make adjustments with your smart phone! And more and more buildings are "looped," that is, installed with Bluetooth-accessible hearing enhancement, if you have compatible aids.

Just like bifocals, hearing aids require some time for your brain to adjust. It speeds the process if the new user puts them in each morning on rising and takes them out each night at bedtime. The good news is that there appears to be a certain brain plasticity at all ages. We accommodate new data input, just like Google remembers your searches and you needn't work so hard to reach a site you are looking for if you have been there before. Our brains are capable of great change whatever our age, if we don't wait *too* long. One of the things I missed the most during the pandemic was hearing children's voices. Hearing aids make that much easier. I took notes the first week I had mine and want to share some with you:

Pro: Birdsong! One reason I chose to get hearing aids was to hear birds. Indeed, now I can hear them much better. Even the sounds of the terns are vivid; they sound much like pterodactyls. How do I know what pterodactyls sound like? I've seen *Jurassic Park*!

The high voices of children are much easier to decipher and the same goes for foreign accents.

Con: I hear my dog's rabies and id tags clittering against each other. Who knew?

To summarize

How can we keep fit and enjoy it? Let me count the ways:

- **Find what you actually like** that will keep you fit and do it vigorously **at least three times a week for at least an hour**

- **Eat what you want when you want—in small quantities**—and avoid meat and processed foods

- **Drink alcohol if you like—in very small quantities**, defined as a single daily dose of 1.5 ounces of spirits, 12 ounces of beer, or 5 ounces of wine

- **Have a dog**

- **Have an exercise buddy**

- **Participate in a walking group**

- **Stick to an exercise class** with music you like

- **Create an exercise routine** and stick to it religiously

- **Try new forms of working out**

- **Ask your friends what they like**

- **Ask your doctor about recommendations**
- **Take the stairs**
- **Park farther from your destination**
- **Look at your friends who died prematurely** (any age before 80). Of about three dozen friends in my UW graduating class of 1970 who I still know, those who didn't quit smoking, and those seriously overweight, are all dead. (At last count, 4; the oldest person in this cohort is 73.)
- **Wear a helmet during active sports**

But even if your body is as fit as possible, what else gives your life life? Let's explore that together in the next chapter.

6

Meaning and Purpose

"If there's one thing I've learned in my years on this planet, it's that the happiest and most fulfilled people are those who devoted themselves to something bigger and more profound than merely their own self-interest."

These are the words of John Glenn, astronaut, and former U.S. Senator, spoken in 1997, when he donated his personal and Senate papers to Ohio State University. He was making the gift in order, he said, to encourage young people's enthusiasm for public service.

A life well-lived is one in which there is purpose, and that purpose is meaningful. We can't all become astronauts or Senators, but I remember a bed-bound resident in a mediocre nursing home who understood what it took to be happy and fulfilled. When I interviewed her as part of a research study, the first thing she wanted to talk about was her knitting, proudly showing me the weeks' worth of adorable caps for newborn babies that she regularly donated to a nearby hospital. Her scores on the two measures I was using to gauge quality of life were both high. In extreme old age, with severe disabilities, and in a challenging environment, she created meaning and perceived a high quality of life. She lived a life of meaning and purpose.

A friend's brother recently retired and discovered that there was nothing he found truly engrossing. Working for many years in a job where he was part of a team, he had found purpose in the work, as well as meaning and friendship in that group of colleagues. Without them, he felt lost. How would you advise this person to find meaning?

What I would say to him, and to you, the reader of this book, is: *Actively contemplate what you care about passionately.* Or, as Joseph Campbell wrote, "Follow your bliss." Jane Goodall had a passion for learning about chimpanzees. She went to Africa at the age of 26 with no experience, but she had encouragement (and a small stipend) from brilliant anthropologist Louis Leakey, as well as a supportive family. Her work was initially criticized for anthropomorphizing her field subjects. *Don't give them names*, she was told. *Don't ascribe human emotions to them.* It took time, but her dramatic scientific findings proved groundbreaking. When she witnessed the chimpanzees modifying stems and grasses to use them as tools, scholars had to redefine what it means to be human, previously thought of as the only tool-making primate. Still living a life of meaning and purpose in her eighties, she continues to work as a conservation activist.

No matter what

I suggest that paid *and* unpaid work at all ages of life, no matter how busy, how poor, how discouraged you are, can be meaningful, satisfying, and productive. The happiest children I've met have purposeful tasks and altruistic opportunities. Busy parents of small children often volunteer at their schools and sports programs. For myself, I want to be remembered for my teaching, my volunteer work, and my environmental restoration.

We all have good times and hard times. How we deal with leisure and pleasure is at least as important as how we cope with hardship. Nevertheless, sometimes it is the hardest times that we remember with pride. An exercise in meaning that I recommend is writing your obituary. It appears to me to be a wake-up call if all you can think to write is that you loved cooking, TV, and jigsaw puzzles.

Talking on the phone weekly with my friend Maria was a large part of my social support survival during the pandemic. I am thankful for her intelligence, her friendship, and her spirit.

Just weeks before COVID lockdown began, Maria had a gargantuan above-the-knee amputation of her left leg. A Ph.D. health educator, she is a super trouper who knew exactly what her bone cancer meant. Indomitable, she named her prosthesis 'Rover' and adhered religiously to her physical therapy regime. She had to deal not only with her amputation but also with her move to a place much removed from her normal friends and groups, and she faced these multiple challenges with grace. Now living in a retirement community where everyone was confined to their apartments for long stretches during COVID-19, she kept engaged and helped lead a committee that set pandemic policy for their large and diverse population. Maria exemplifies purpose and meaning by helping others, reaching out, and dealing head-on with disaster.

A vital component

A life with meaning and purpose is clearly a component in staying out of a nursing home and living a good old age. MacArthur 'Genius Grant' recipients John Rowe and Robert Kahn, in their meta-analysis of aging well, called it engagement. Their book, Su*ccessful Aging*, published in 1998, was prescient in analyzing what are now often thought of as common-sense factors for a healthy, fulfilling old age. When they began to research the human life span, they examined not just the number of years, but the quality of life in old age, and much of their book predicted what has now been proven in research again and again.

While it is extremely difficult to define and measure quality of life, it is universally agreed that it is vitally important. When I did a study to quantify it in nursing homes, I used two instruments. The first was a complex set of questions (originally designed for people with cancer) that measured a wide range of variables, from physical environment, quality of food and care, to sex life and social life. These were then cross tallied with how important an individual considered the variables. For example, a person would be asked how satisfied he or she was with the living arrangements (usually their room). Then the person was asked, "How important to you is your room?" It was amazing how similar individuals in similar rooms would rate the rooms quite differently, as well as having wildly different scores on the importance of the physical setting. Some people found the smallish room horrible but didn't think it important; others found very similar rooms delightful and thought it very important.

The second questionnaire basically asked the question, "How would you describe your quality of life? Very high, high, low, or very low." Forcing people to choose a degree of high or low, rather than giving them a middle option, gave a more functional result. The totals correlated with the individuals' ratings on the other quality of life instrument. While it wasn't totally clear exactly what I was actually measuring (given how problematic it is to define and quantify quality of life), it certainly had something to do with personal perception of general well-being.

When I then asked participants, "What gives your life meaning?", there were many excellent answers: volunteering, working, teaching, grandchildren, spiritual belief system, to name just a few.

However, we are not talking about hobbies such as jigsaw puzzles. A purposeful life is different. How so? For example, sitting alone in your kitchen working a jigsaw puzzle is boredom prevention. Teenagers sitting down with seniors at a youth center or senior center to do jigsaw puzzles together—that would be purposeful. Many people find joy, meaning, and purpose in their families and grandchildren. Some do not.

There are those who find joy, meaning, and purpose in their religion. Others do not. My late husband strongly believed that the planet would be better off if no one believed in an afterlife. He felt that what we have in our lifetimes is all we have, ever. Think of the wars that might never have happened, the environments that might never have been destroyed, the families and countries never torn apart because of religion with a belief in an afterlife. What if a promise of virgins in heaven did not inspire suicide bombers and people did good for its own sake rather than an eternal reward? Understanding the harm we do to the planet now and acting to reverse global warming, means that future humans—including our grandchildren—will undoubtedly have a better life.

I remember when I was volunteering for hospice as a friendly visitor for a couple in their nineties. The wife had severe dementia, but I discovered that she greatly enjoyed the newspaper being read to her. She especially liked the comics and advice columns, over which we would laugh and exclaim. "Thank you so much," her husband said to me one day. "You will get your reward in heaven." I didn't have the chutzpah to say, "I'm getting my reward right now—sharing happiness and fun." For me, heaven is not the reward. Spiritual well-being is nurtured by kindness. Compassion brings joy. These are immediate rewards.

Doing good brings good. As the Dalai Lama said, "Be kind whenever possible. It is always possible."

I never imagined that I would find myself trying to write about the meaning of life. But just like quality of life, about which I have written extensively, most agree that it is important, though few agree on how to achieve a meaningful life. Again, we can construe certain commonalities, but your quality might not be my quality; your meaning might not be my meaning.

Since viewpoints vary so wildly on this nebulous subject, I asked my philosophical friend and colleague Sandy Sabersky to write about meaning and purpose for this book and she was kind enough to do so. Here is what Sandy shares with us:

Quietly listen to the peaceful, inner "I"

A few years ago, I listened to a program from *The New York Times,* 'The Field: The Fight for Voting Rights in Florida,' which included an interview with a man named Julius Irving who was working to register ex-felons to vote. A former felon himself, this project—as well as the rest of his life—was very challenging and complicated, but at that moment, Julius said that he felt freedom. Why? Because "I'm doing the right thing. I'm doing it in the right way, and I feel like my natural self."

To me, this sums up finding meaning and purpose in life.

Before they died, I asked my elderly parents what their philosophy of life was. I was surprised by their answers. My mother said, "Life is one obstacle after another—when the obstacle comes, you just jump over it." At first, I couldn't understand this. My mother's spiritual life came first for her. I knew her life goal, to be to get closer to God, or the Universal Reality. But, day to day, things invariably get in your way. Small things, like when her neighbor complained that my mother's keeping the bathroom light on at night kept her awake. This neighbor's bedroom was across from my mother's bathroom and the light bothered her when she was trying to sleep. My mother, however, being nearly blind, needed the light on in the bathroom at night for safety. Well, you have to deal with this. It's an obstacle, if a small one. And there are many considerations in dealing with this in a way that is in harmony with one's values and beliefs.

There are big obstacles also that likely led my mother to have this philosophy of life. She had to leave Germany in Hitler's time and she fled to Switzerland, Cuba, and finally the United States with many adventures/obstacles along the way. The thing I noticed in watching my parents age is that the obstacles don't go away. It seems only fair that with aging and wisdom one should have a decline in obstacles, but it is not so. My mother continued to negotiate the obstacles presented to her with grace and courage, and in accordance with her beliefs.

My father's answer to this question was, "luck." He said he was lucky that he was able to get out of Germany (not *un*lucky that he had to leave Germany), lucky to go to the schools he did, and lucky to have married my mother. He was grateful for what he had, and indeed, his last words to my sister and me, who took care of him in his final days, were, "Thank you."

So, what does it mean to have 'meaning and purpose' in our lives? How do we find the rudder that steers the boat in the direction we want it to go? And indeed, how do we find the goal, the destination to aim for? What is our philosophy of life?

My advice? Listen to yourself. Listen to that quiet, inner "I." Listen to what you feel compelled to do and then wonder, *Why am I compelled to do this?* Ask yourself, *Does this work feel good?*

There is no right answer to what our meaning or purpose *should* be, only that all parts of our selves aim to move in the same direction. We really aren't different people at different times. We may be in different situations, but if we are aiming to be kind, then, despite the obstacles, we can do that in all situations.

If we look at ourselves from the inside out, we can see that the inside, our innermost part, contains what is most important. That interior part will tell us what we value most. Is it truth, kindness, connectedness, thinking of others, or joy itself? Moving outwards, we find our hearts, that part of us that feels love and compassion; that part that wants to give to others. Continuing further outward, we find the intellect that is creative and wills itself to work to make change or do good in the world. Then comes the mind with its sense perceptions, and finally, the outside, our bodies themselves. We often make the mistake of thinking the outside is the most important. We have become accustomed to our bodies and value them, though we know they don't last forever. Rather, in thinking about our life's purpose, let's think about the inner layers, as well as the body.

For some, a goal of making money is important.

It makes it possible to feed one's family or provide for an education. For some with physical or mental health challenges, a goal of taking care of one's physical or mental health is of primary importance, for without the body or mind, it becomes difficult to work. Our goals may change also. Maybe my health improves, and I strive for an education—either secular or spiritual. The idea is that we continue to learn and grow; that is what we are here for. We can learn to be kinder, less jealous, more accepting, more aware of our own faults than those of other's.

As an experiment, I asked my daughter to post the following incomplete statements on Facebook: *I find meaning in life by*_____, and *The purpose of my life is*_____.

Over thirty persons responded to her request to fill in the blanks. Though it's not a random sample, I was pleasantly surprised that when it came to meaning and purpose, most of the respondent's answers had to do with the deeper parts of themselves—their essence, their heart, their intellect, and their creativity.

Here are some of their answers.

I find meaning in life by:
- Using my brain to do good things
- To thrive and grow and pass it on
- Love one another and share compassion
- Trying to make the world a better place
- Creating, questioning, educating
- Making lasting and meaningful connections
- Giving
- Respecting and nurturing each child's destiny
- Breaking intergenerational cycles

- Living authentically
- Helping heal and uplift
- Spreading joy

The purpose of my life is:
- Being with others, connecting, empathizing with others
- To raise two amazing daughters
- Giving, nurturing, spreading goodness
- Using my strengths and gifts to help others
- Creating art, feeling gratitude, tuning into the infinite universe
- To be in relationship with the earth and my beloveds, being alive together
- Being present
- Deeply listening
- Being loving
- Being myself and sharing with others
- Bringing joy and love to my family and friends
- Slowing down and listening
- Making connections
- Learning tools to help relieve unnecessary suffering
- Helping people in grief
- Singing, storytelling, dancing
- Connecting, creating, teaching, savoring
- Creating and being vulnerable
- Being kind and deepening connection in a community

Some of their answers related to their essence, the deepest part of themselves—loving, listening, being present, bringing joy. Some related to their heart level—caring for others, being grateful for a new day, sharing with others, raising children, empathizing, helping to heal. Others had to do with the intellect and creativity—using my brain to do good things, teaching, questioning, creating. Those who responded were mostly young people. What stood out for me is that there is so much optimism, such sincerity and goodness in the answers.

After living a long life, we may feel we didn't accomplish all we set out to do, or our marriage or childrearing or career didn't happen as we thought it should, or didn't happen at all. Maybe our health wasn't as good as we hoped. But perhaps the questions we ask ourselves by looking back can help us appreciate where we are. *Can I feel good that I have become kinder, more thoughtful of others, less selfish, more giving? Have I worked to improve my character, am I doing my best? Have I done my work, whatever that may be, with a good attitude?* Life is not usually what we expect, but if we can grow, expand our thoughts, and try to be better, that seems to me a good start.

All parts of our body/mind complex are important—it's important to get exercise, to eat well, etc., but to find meaning and purpose in our lives, we must listen most to the one who is steering the boat. That one will be honest with us. If we listen carefully, it will tell us what direction is right for us, it will tell us in what direction we are headed, and perhaps help guide us past some obstacles we need to jump over along the way.

Life is a wonderful opportunity to learn and grow, even as we experience pain and suffering. I have this image of the ocean beating down on rocks and pieces of glass. Beating down and beating down. Over time, the rocks become smooth pebbles and the glass, with its rounded edges, we pick up in delight and call sea glass.

It is helpful, with age, if we are able, to bear with the challenges that come. The body ages, relationships may become strained, money may be tight. We will get beaten down, just as if the waves are pounding upon us. Through this, somehow, we hang on to our deep beliefs and values. And, just like the sea glass, we will be filled with light and soft edges.

I am grateful to Sandy for her inspiring and useful insights. Writing this book, for me, is an act of listening to my "I." Sometimes the writing is painful and brings me to tears. Sometimes I don't want to write it at all. Other times I feel I can't stop myself. It was helpful for me to read Sandy's kind and true words. I hope that is so for you too.

7

Interconnected, Interwoven Intersections

Action and activism that can reach beyond our lifetime

The things I care about most are the climate catastrophe and improving the quality of life in old age, concepts that profoundly intersect. It is clear that if the first is not promptly addressed, fewer and fewer humans will be able to *have* an old age worth living.

What does a healthy, clean, green, and peaceful planet have to do with quality of life? It has *everything* to do with quality of life—at all ages.

Are people in drought zones aging well? Are children in war zones destined for a long and peaceful life? Is our crowded and overheated planet going to support decent lives a hundred years from now, if the planet continues on its present track?

As the planet boils, quality of life declines, health suffers. Quality of life is worse on a planet that has more frequent, unpredictable, and violent storms and fires. A planet where tides are rising. Where air gets dirtier and water scarcer. The droughts and increasing scarcity of farmland precipitate wars. At the very least, your insurance costs will increase dramatically in your lifetime.

How lucky we were, like everyone before us, to be born on a planet that was healthy. People in my generation are the last to have grown up in a world not deeply impacted by climate change. But our children and grandchildren are in peril. Humans have wrecked this planet and those next generations will pay the price— living with the climate catastrophe after my generation is dead. They are also those who, I hope, will repair it.

This chapter is being completed as COVID limps to a lessening of illness, reduced deaths, and fewer restrictions. At the same time, Russia is bombing civilians in Ukraine, and the once almost forgotten possibility of nuclear war hangs over us again.

These, along with inflation, mass shootings, and the high price of gas, have pushed the clear threat of climate catastrophe to the background. Nevertheless, the knowledge of it looms large for the many scientists, educators, and informed citizens who know this cataclysm is real. We also know that we can—and must— do something about it. But if we are too tightly wrapped in doom, such fear could inspire paralysis.

Is it possible that you are still unconvinced that the planet *has* significantly warmed since the Industrial Revolution, and *is* continuing its drastic warming? The NASA Goddard Institute for Space Studies tells us that the scientific consensus is clear: *climate.nasa.gov/ scientific-consensus*

- Average global temperatures have increased by 2.2° Fahrenheit since 1880.

- The Arctic has warmed by more than 4° since the 1960s.
- On June 29, 2021, the Northwest United States experienced record-breaking temperatures — some as much as 10° above the previous records.
- The extreme heat and low tides caused the death of millions—*millions*—of marine life creatures, such as shellfish and salmon. Instead of the fresh smell of the ocean, one was hit by the putrid smell of death for days on the Pacific coast in 2021.

Al Gore was right. In 2006, when his film, *An Inconvenient Truth*, was released, Mr. Gore was lampooned by the right, and even ridiculed by some of his environmentalist colleagues for being so alarmist. Now the world has incontrovertible evidence. The planet

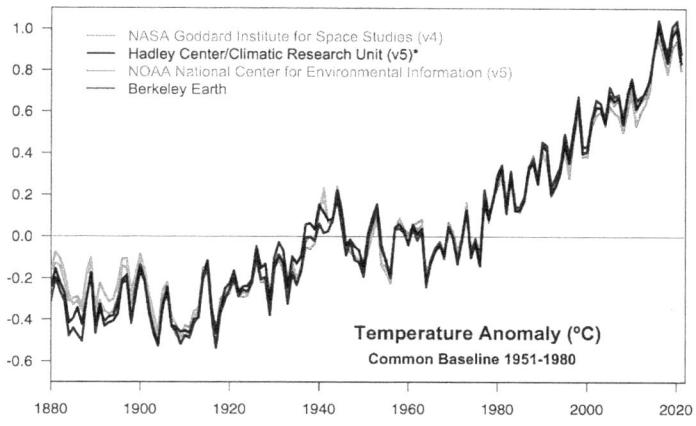

Temperature data showing rapid warming in the past few decades, the latest data going up to 2021. According to NASA, 2016 and 2020 are tied for the warmest year since 1880, continuing a long-term trend of rising global temperatures. The eight most recent years have been the warmest. Credit: NASA's Goddard Institute for Space Studies

is heating up to an alarming degree, and its effects are being felt globally. It is ruining lives, destroying homes, negatively impacting food production, businesses, economies. And it is proven to be human caused.

All who take science seriously, along with those around the world who daily witness the overwhelming evidence—flooding, fires, heat waves, and the polar ice caps melting even faster than the direst warnings predicted—are convinced.

In their April 2021 article, *The Science of Climate Change Explained: Facts, Evidence and Proof, The New York Times* makes a clear, cogent, and well-documented analysis of science—including important insights into the sources of deliberate misinformation. According to an apolitical AARP June 2021 article, *What You Need to Know About Climate Change (aarp.org)*, the rising temperatures have increased so rapidly that warming threatens not just you, but perhaps more importantly, your legacy as a human, not to mention the lives of your children and grandchildren.

Then there's COVID, to which the issue of climate change is connected in multiple ways. As habitat shrinks from rising seas and encroachment of human habitation and farming, wild creatures—such as bats, rats, and the viruses, bacteria, and danger they spread—will increasingly invade human-dominated areas. As cities grow hotter and more crowded, diseases will spread more rapidly. Arable land and other resources are becoming increasingly scarce. Conflicts continue to rise. As the same April 2021 *New York Times* article, says, "...warmer weather is aiding the spread of infectious diseases and the vectors that transmit them, like ticks and mosquitoes." There are scientists who believe that the COVID-19 pandemic is linked to a crowded "wet market" where wild animals were sold as delicacies. We may never know the complete truth about the origin of the virus, but we do know that crowding wild creatures into smaller and smaller habitats on an overcrowded planet is causing horrific damage on many levels.

The United States, ostensibly the world's richest country, has had the *highest* rates of COVID cases per capita in the world. Residents and staff in skilled care facilities had far more deaths and positive cases than the general population. And there is hard data about how the isolation and loneliness experienced during COVID exacerbated mental and physical health declines precipitously in long-term care settings.

Not only are older people at great risk of contracting, dying from, or being left with lasting disabilities from the virus, but so are their care-providers—who are often not white, or well-educated, or well-to-do. Being threatened with potentially deadly disease on a daily basis in your job is cruel and unusual punishment in any culture. And for the residents, it is a heartbreaking thought that so many died alone in a nursing home without family or loved ones to hold their hands.

These concerns intersect with those of all the other chapters of this book. How can life have deep meaning if your grandchildren are doomed to a dying planet trashed by previous generations? What can we as individuals and as a society meaningfully do to mitigate the disaster happening as we speak? And how is a clean and healthy planet going to keep you out of a nursing home?

It is possible to find a 'good' nursing home, but, in

general, ending one's life in what is licensed as skilled care is a fate most would wish to avoid. Those of us who are old enough to be at risk of being put into such a setting, and young enough to live to see global warming get even worse, are more likely to become disabled and need help. Breathing toxic air could contribute to damaging your respiratory system to such an extent that you may need skilled care. The great Salt Lake in Utah has become "an environmental nuclear bomb."

I did not want this book to be political. Aging knows no political party. But it is not possible to leave politics out of the discussion today. If you disavow global warming, because it is politically convenient to do so, you are wearing dangerous blinders.

The real question is, what can humans, on a personal, political, and world scale, do? Mr. Gore wrote with considerable optimism in a December 2020 *New York Times* article entitled *Where I Find Hope*: "Even as the climate crisis rapidly worsens, scientists, engineers and business leaders are making use of stunning advances in technology to end the world's dependence on fossil fuels far sooner than was hoped possible."

One useful book is Paul Greenberg's *50 Simple Ways to Trim Your Carbon Footprint*. This small, affordable paperback is crammed with good ideas and available at most libraries. For example, most of us know that being a vegetarian, especially being vegan, is far less damaging to the planet (and often your heart). But Greenberg encourages you to be a 'picky plant eater.' Food processing and transportation can make vegetables more carbon costly than those raised and sold locally in season. He also makes the point that frozen foods can be more carbon friendly than trucking in fresh foods. Tap water is by far the cheapest beverage we can drink.

Choose a wedding venue close to home and friends. Buy fewer clothes and shop recycled. Producing a single cotton shirt uses more than 713 gallons of water. Invest in a forest by donating to your local land trust or nature conservancy.

To quote Mr. Greenberg, not having a child is the "single most powerful way Americans can reduce their carbon footprint…" This is why, while some people lament the low birthrate, I celebrate it. While it does make access to home caregivers even more challenging—because the ratio of old people to young people is so high—my hope is that it will help open the door to our welcoming refugees and immigrants, among them people who find genuine love and satisfaction from caring for others.

I have been a well-documented tree hugger since childhood. I spent my youth roaming the first, second, and third growth forests of the Pacific Northwest. When I first visited the rainforest in the Olympic National Park, I embraced the moss- and fern-festooned trees like they were my sisters. It turns out that undisturbed or minimally disturbed old growth and other mature forests are on the front lines of combating catastrophic global warming. Trees are the front-line soldiers holding on to carbon dioxide. A heart-rending *New York Times* article, *Climate Change and California's Favorite Trees*, contains some devastating photos of the damage already done by fire in that state. According to experts, while historically these trees were practically fireproof, now wildfires, aided by climate change and invasive non-native grasses, are taking out these mighty giants. There are scientific predictions that Glacier National Park may, by the year 2030, be robbed of the year-round ice for which it is named.

I don't only lament the threatened polar bears and adorable seals and otters. I fear for the future of humankind.

But there is also hope for that future. It lies in the fact that the economic and ethical dilemmas of using fossil fuels are becoming clearer. Wind and solar power are becoming increasingly competitive. Companies like Exxon and BP are rethinking their profit strategies. It's tragic that the U.S. is absurdly behind in the race to mitigate global warming, but more and more, politicians, economists, and voters are seeing the benefits of exiting a philosophy of denial.

Among these are economists and artists, businesspeople and politicians, who are discussing and envisioning a circular economy that both saves resources and eliminates waste. You can watch a fascinating conversation between the founder of the Ellen MacArthur Foundation, Dame Ellen MacArthur, and others, with *New York Times* reporter Andrew Ross Sorkin, about the question, *Can We Get to Net Zero With a 'Circular' Economic Strategy?*

There is profit to be made in saving the planet. Investing in the future of our children worldwide makes moral and economic sense. Major investors, ranging from the California State Teachers Retirement System to the Church of England, are divesting from fossil fuels. In January 2021, on Inauguration Day, President Biden had the U.S. rejoin the Paris Climate Accord, a move welcomed by many corporations. Bill Ford, the chairman of the Ford Motor Company and the great-grandson of Henry Ford, released a statement, *From Detroit to Paris: It is time for climate progress*, in which he said:

"Climate change is everyone's problem. It is already affecting every person on the planet, whether they realize it or not...We believe that real and lasting change will only come from our will and a commitment to our values on a global scale to do better for our children and grandchildren."

I am aware that, quite possibly, the only people who read this chapter are those who are already worried about the health of the planet. Perhaps that means I am preaching to the choir. But even if that is so, the choir is here because they already believe, so it's not about the preacher changing their minds. But she might give those singers more to sing about.

Seek out and find paths to living in a more carbon-friendly way. Check the EPA's website, *What You Can Do About Climate Change (epa.gov)*. It offers many clear, easy steps to take. Support a cause mitigating climate change, such as reforestation, native plant preservation, nature and science education for children, and many more. Let the petroleum industry know that they must find other ways to provide electricity. Bring your own mug to Starbucks. Unplug your computer, digital devices, and TV when you're not using them. For more suggestions, look at the UC Davis list of *18 Simple Things You Can Do About Climate Change (ucdavis.edu/climate)*. Encourage the removal of fossil fuel subsidies. Vote.

In other words, do what you can. It's all that you can do.

Remember your Resources

While the Kindle version of this book has live links, the print version, of course, does not. But even with live links, it's important to remember that websites come and go. This list presents a few of the most useful search terms, resources, and websites.

Most of the resources in the chapters should be easy to find with key word combination searches, for example, 'aging in place' or 'universal design.' In addition, much new and useful information is published daily online and in print. Define a problem you wish to address and then seek solutions.

But be wary. Anyone can publish anything on the World Wide Web. Many websites are trying to shape your opinions, gain your personal information, or make a sale. Many, but not all, non-profit sites end in '.org'. Many commercial sites end in '.com', but a for-profit website can end in '.org'. Sites with '.edu' tend to be more reliable because they are educational institutions. But even the best information can change or have errors.

Always be vigilant. Don't give out your personal information unless you are certain of a site. How to be absolutely certain? Librarians are generally excellent resources for just about any technical, resource, or information help you may need. But even librarians may be mistaken, so if you have any doubt at all, move on to the next site.

One of my favorite sources is *The New York Times*, especially the Tuesday Science Section, their 'Well' newsletter, and the Weekly Health Quiz.

Here are a few other resources:

AARP Livable Communities "supports the efforts of neighborhoods, towns, cities and rural areas to be great places for people of all ages." Follow the links on their site to subscribe to their weekly newsletter.
aarp.org/livable-communities

Aging in Place provides free online resources for all aspects of aging at home.
aginginplace.org

The National Institute on Aging also provides links and information on their Aging in Place: Growing Older at Home web page.
nia.nih.gov/health/aging-place-growing-older-home

Ashton Applewhite's book, *This Chair Rocks*, traces her journey from apprehensive boomer to pro-aging radical, and in the process debunks myth after myth about late life. She blogs on her website, which also has links and information on combating ageism.
thischairrocks.com

NW Universal Design Council's Environments for All website has much useful information, especially the Home Checklist.
environmentsforall.org

Gray is Green: "An online gathering of older adult Americans aspiring to create a green legacy for the future." *grayisgreen.org*

Invisia accessibility products are sold on many websites and in-person shopping, from Amazon to Lowe's to Walmart.

Old School is an anti-ageism clearing house, which "curates, creates, commissions and disseminates free resources to educate people about ageism and how to end it." *oldschool.info*

Village to Village Network connects community-based, nonprofit, grassroots organizations composed of caring neighbors who want to change the paradigm of aging.
vtvnetwork.org

World Health Organization is working with its Member States at national and local levels to develop age-friendly cities and communities, within the context of the UN Decade of Healthy Aging (2021-2030). *who.int/activities/creating-age-friendly-cities-and-communities*

Acknowledgements

I am lucky indeed to live in a community of writers, artists, and their supporters. These people help us grow with grit, grace, and knowledge.

I would like to acknowledge the many people and community icons who wittingly or unwittingly helped with this book. My apologies to anyone I've forgotten or omitted in this alphabetical list.

I would like to thank: Claudia Anderson, for her comments on titles and content, and Katie Auger, IVC Resource Navigator, resourcedirectorybi.org, who also participated in the "Name that Book" zoom. Michael Bourne, for letting me bounce ideas and road-test a chapter or two. Eagle Harbor Book Company, for being an independent bookstore and jewel in the crown of local readers and writers.

I greatly appreciate that Cheryl Chuka Mauer, Windemere, took me and my spouse around to multiple condos knowing it was research for *To Move or Stay Put.* Ruth Neuwald Falcon is a superb editor with an eye for the truth—thank you so much. Dorothy K. Foster, brilliant and beloved attorney, contributed considerably to Chapter 2, making it clear and legal.

I cannot forget Tressa Johnson, the librarian's librarian; Omie Kerr, who told me, "This book is not about staying out of a nursing home"; and Joan Pearson, neighbor, writer, and friend.

Thank you, Reed Price, for making Bainbridge an island for all ages.

I am profoundly glad I found Joy Rubin, of Joy Rubin Creative LLC, a patient and hard-working book designer; and Sandy Sabersky, a collaborator who made the *Meaning and Purpose* chapter much more meaningful and purposeful.

Although she didn't know it until now, I deeply appreciate Cynthia Sears, without whom Bainbridge Island would be a much less art-friendly, book-friendly, pet-friendly, elder-friendly community.

Andy Tadesse—everyone should be so fortunate as to have a financial advisor like Andy. And thank you, LT Yoson, for giving ideas and joining the title discussion.

Jeannette Franks, Ph.D., is a passionate gerontologist who, for over 25 years, taught ethics, grief and loss, and courses on geriatrics and gerontology for the University of Washington.

Franks' published books include, *To Move or To Stay Put: A Guide for Your Last Decades*, as well as, *Washington Retirement Communities*. She says, "After many years in the field of aging and long-term care, I've seen many mistakes and many wise choices. In my books I give tools and frameworks for better decision making."

Much of this book is based on her talks,"7 Actions to Take to Avoid a Nursing Home."

Dr. Franks is also recognized for her native plant and forest restoration.

CPSIA information can be obtained
at www.ICGtesting.com
Printed in the USA
LVHW080256310523
748356LV00001B/118